A Guide
for Midlife

Navigating the
Six Universal Crises

by McKenzie Magee

GEM PUBLISHING

Illustrations © Glenn Wolff

Published by Gem Publishing, P.O.Box 1453, Cheyenne, WY 82003

For information, please contact McKenzie Magee at www.guideformidlife.com

Printed and bound in the United States, first printing 2009
Cover and book design by Saxon Design, Inc., Traverse City, MI

CONTENTS

DEDICATION

To my fellow travelers,
known and unknown to me.

Journeys bring power and love back into you.
If you can't go somewhere, move in the passageways of
the self. They are like shafts of light, always changing,
and you change when you explore them.

Rumi

INTRODUCTION

To know the road ahead, ask those coming back.

~Chinese Proverb

I wish I'd had a guidebook like this when I was going through my midlife journey. Coming back, I wrote this book so that you may know the road ahead.

WHEN DOES MIDLIFE ACTUALLY OCCUR?

For the purposes of this book, midlife is that span of your life from age thirty-five to fifty-six.

WHAT EXACTLY IS MIDLIFE?

Midlife is the time during which life gives you specifically timed opportunities to find your authenticity, power, clarity, stature, balance and beliefs, and contribution. It also presents you with a second call to find your higher life purpose if you have not yet found it. The word midlife is most often linked with the word crisis. For most of us, a crisis is an unwelcome experience, mostly because it feels like an intrusion rather than an invitation. Yet the Encarta World English Dictionary defines crisis as "a time when something very important for the future happens or is decided." *A Guide for Midlife* helps you to make key decisions in the midst of, and even beyond midlife events—decisions that will make the difference between just surviving and purposefully thriving for the rest of your life.

WHY AM I HERE? WHAT IS MY PURPOSE?

As one who began to ask these questions around the age of thirty-six, I happened upon the inner path to the outer fulfillment of my higher life purpose. This is the same path taught by indigenous and spiritual teachers, both contemporary and ancient. Now, as a counselor, guide, and teacher to those who seek the answer to these same questions, I offer this book. In its pages you will find many gems to collect for your midlife journey, a time in which life offers you the opportunity to transform yourself to match the beauty of your spirit.

M.C. Richards, essayist, poet, potter, and painter, said that knowledge of the path could not be substituted for putting one foot in front of the other. This book is not a substitute for the steps that only you can take through midlife, but your walk will be made easier with the guidance given here.

Just getting through midlife does not guarantee you a successful journey. Commitment to an open mind, motivation to stay awake, courage to persist, common sense to obey the signs, and willingness to take the lessons you learn into the rest of your life make it so.

- If you are approaching midlife, this guide can help you plan and prepare for it.

- If you are currently between the ages of thirty-five and fifty-one, keep this book in your backpack at all times!

- If you know others who are making the journey, the information here will help you to better understand them.

- If you are past midlife, this book will give you insight into what was actually happening during that period, and then give you some useful items to reclaim in order to thrive on the road ahead. Get ready to have a few "aha!" moments.

As you read, keep only that which is useful to you. Don't be surprised if, as you change in wonderful ways, you uncover new information, insight, and inspiration in these pages. That's the great thing about growth and transformation—it always lets in more light.

Each chapter of this guide has eight sections:

Travel Details

This is the first page of each chapter. Here you will find The Territory, Your Travel Group and Approximate Age, Time in Transit, What to Pack, What to Leave Behind, The Weather Forecast, and the Mantra. Please refer to How to Use this Guide to locate your Travel Group.

Travel Itinerary

This is a concise distillation of knowledge that has come from ancient sages, contemporary teachers, and my own experience. The information given here is timeless—and universal to all people; it is rooted in why we have always used the heavens to help us navigate. Where am I? Where do I wish to go from here? How do I get there? The answers to these questions are in this guide.

I look upon and use the astrological birth chart—what I term throughout as "the life map"—as a pact between an individual and the source of life. This map, a kind of blueprint, is drawn from the exact date, place, and time of your birth, the moment that the breath of life draws itself through your human form.

Through the millennia, in both Eastern and Western cultures, wise counselors have guided countless individuals from all walks and ways of life with the information contained in the birth chart by interpreting its symbolic language. In respect of human relationship to the cosmos, they regard objects (planets) in the universe "above" as symbolically reflecting events on earth "below." At the exquisite and matchless moment of your birth, each planet above is precisely positioned to symbolically reflect your life map onto the stage of your life here on earth below. Again, the exact confluence of your birth and the position of the planets reflect the pact between you and the Source. This pact, your higher life purpose, unfolds into the events and circumstances of your life.

Astrologers, as masters of symbolism, also regard planets as archetypes—a set of characteristics—that are reflected in both your personal life and the collective lives of all human beings. For example, the planet Uranus reflects the characteristics of change, freedom, vision, and technology, to name a few. Therefore, during your Crisis of Authenticity, the time in your life that Uranus is astronomically and symbolically involved, you will find many aspects of its symbolism in your life as events involving change, freedom, vision, and more.

The planets in our heavens orbit in predictable cycles and mirror your own life cycles. Midlife is one such life cycle. When you enter midlife, certain events (crises!) occur. Because we know that specific planetary alignments occur at precise and predictable times, we can determine exactly when each midlife crisis will occur. Where there is crisis, there is opportunity. This guide will tell you when each of your midlife opportunities will occur and how to navigate them.

In short, I describe the Second Call and the six midlife crises of Authenticity, Power, Clarity, Stature, Balance and Beliefs, and Contribution according to their perfect synchronization with the complementary planetary positions. Best of all, you don't have to understand the science of astrology in order to experience its accuracy—simply observe the events of your life against the backdrop of the information in this guide.

NOTE: Throughout each Travel Itinerary section of the book, I use the word Life in reference to the Source—that Source which bestows life. Please feel free to substitute your own name according to your preference or tradition, be it God, Spirit, Divine Mind, Creator, Universal Intelligence, etc.

What's in your map?

As a blueprint of your life, the map contains the possibilities of your life-to-be, as well as your strengths, challenges, and your higher life purpose.

Where can you find your map?

The map resides in your heart, the home of your Higher Self. Some individuals don't know their map exists, while others do. Some keep their map in a back pocket and never refer to it. Some refer to their map only when they are lost. Everyone, including you, has a map.

If you want to acquire a hard copy of your map, a competent astrologer can draw one up for you by using the date, place, and time of your birth. Even though they each contain the same information, always use your hard copy map in concert with your heart map.

Why is your map important?

The map gives you the precise guidance of a Global Positioning System; it can show you where the potholes and potentials of your life are. It also possesses the accuracy of a fine chronometer to give you a great sense of timing, since it is synchronized with universal timing. Most importantly, your map gives you free will to choose the low road, the high road, or any road in between.

Sights and Sounds

Your outer reality reflects your inner state. If you choose to change your inner landscape during midlife, your outer landscape will become a reflection of that. During midlife, you are offered better scenery for your life, if you are willing to receive it. The list of Sights and Sounds for each crisis gives you a life-long menu of choices to take with you.

Traveling Companions

In this section you'll meet your traveling companions. These are people, most of whom I have met in my travels, who graciously agreed to share their midlife stories. They live in every corner of the world and come from all walks and ways of life. You have a lot of company—join them and enjoy the journey together!

McKenzie's Journal

I offer myself as one of your midlife traveling companions by opening my personal journals to you. You will see from my experiences that life is messy, but it is also miraculous. If you read each of the Journals in the order that they are given, you'll get a real-life sense of how each midlife challenge is meant to foster exactly what you'll need to thrive for the rest of your life. Even though my life follows a spiritual path, the path you choose is equally perfect.

The Illustrations

These contain scenes from my outer life and inner life (my Higher Self sessions) that Glenn Wolff rendered in collaboration with me. Each image has connections to McKenzie's Journal and Norbu's Parable. As you read these sections in each chapter, you might wish to refer to these illustrations to Technicolor your experience.

Norbu's Parables

A parable is a teaching story. It has different meaning for each person. But as you grow and change, the same parable yields more of its secrets to you.

Norbu Sherpa is the personification of my Higher Self that spontaneously appeared in one of my first "inner journeys." The Higher Self, the pure reflection of your spiritual self, is that aspect which connects you to the Source.

Norbu's Parables are the actual transcripts of my inner work, and which were scribed for me by skilled facilitators as I verbalized the experiences that took place within me. During each of my midlife crises, I went within to access my highest possible guidance. Norbu showed up every time to provide it. In each parable, Shaypa is actually I, McKenzie; for an easier read for you, I chose the name Shaypa. This is not an actual name, but a Tibetan word meaning to know, understand, realize, or to be conscious and aware. Norbu, in Tibetan, means gem.

I have experienced more than one hundred fifty such "inner parables" over the last twenty years of my life. The transcripts, now quite a stack of them, continue to reveal new insights and meaning. As personal as they are to me, I have found them to also be universal; every person on this planet is capable of contacting images, teachings, and perspectives specific to their needs. The great sages and teachers throughout time accessed their teaching parables from the same place—the Source within. And it is one's Higher Self that can provide the connection.

CHERRY'S POEMS

On December 1, 2003, I landed in Nelson, New Zealand, with a suitcase, my tennis gear and a plan to explore this magical country for four months. I rented a cottage, bought a fourth-hand Honda, and located the tennis clubs.

The third week into my stay, I introduced myself to the Tuesday morning women's tennis group at the Richmond Tennis Club. I was warmly welcomed and even invited to a fortieth birthday party for Jan, one of the players, at the home of Val and Rob Earle.

Val and Rob next invited me to spend the Christmas holidays at their family retreat in the Marlborough Sounds. Sailing out of Havelock through the Sounds to Paradise Bay on Rob's boat, the beauty of this region of New Zealand left me speechless (and I'm Irish-Italian!)

On Christmas Eve, Rob, Val, and I found in our conversation many shared experiences and love of Spirit. We drank champagne and talked late into the night. When I went to sleep, I felt as if I had arrived home halfway around the world.

On Christmas day, Rob's mother, Cherry, arrived. Although we'd never met before, I felt that I "knew" her. I didn't know it then, but that connection was about to yield its secret. The next day, December 26, 2003, Cherry turned eighty-nine.

Back in Nelson after the holidays, Rob and Val invited me to live with them for my remaining three months. I became a member of the family and, as such, was included in Sunday evening dinners at Cherry's house. On my first visit there, Rob asked Cherry to read one of her poems after dinner.

Out came an old notebook that held the fragile onionskin paper on which she had typed her poems so many years ago. Cherry turned to a page at random and read aloud to us. As I listened, a strange feeling came over me. She read another. Suddenly, my eyes widened as I realized that both poems were perfect metaphors for two of the chapters in this book, which I was just beginning to write at the time. I asked her to read a third. It fit yet another of the chapters. And so it was: poems written long ago by a Capricorn woman of New Zealand proved to be perfect, poetic match to every chapter of a book just begun by a Capricorn woman of the United States. What I had felt on first meeting Cherry certainly seemed like destiny's hand.

For the remainder of my stay in New Zealand, one of my favorite things to do was to visit Cherry for tea and conversation about all matters spiritual. As of this writing, "young Ched," as her family fondly calls her, has surpassed her Fifth Call, at age 93. I am forever grateful for her generosity in offering her poems of divine brevity and beauty to this book. May you happily realize in them the unity of all experience across time and space.

ACKNOWLEDGEMENTS

It took me fourteen midlife years to live what then it took me another six years to write about in this book. I am deeply grateful to those who helped me along the way, and to those who helped me to bring this book to you.

TYPING AND TRANSCRIPTION

Kaye Zumbach: who typed countless pages of research material, text, and Higher Self transcripts.

Jean Lane: who gave me her time free of charge because she considered it her contribution.

Linda Sioen: who was unbelievably efficient, and that's worth a lot when you need to get to your destination on time.

Sandy Erickson: whose personal and professional repertoire of diligence, skill, and kindness is an example.

ADVICE AND CRITIQUE

Nancy Kotting: when a real writer tells you, "this is awesome!" that's all you need to keep going.

Kathleen Smith: who showed up at the coffeehouse at the exact right moments to give me important feedback.

Beverly Hill Peshaba: who cried all over the pages of the first draft of the Authenticity chapter, because her own life was in there. Thanks for the truth of your tears, Bev.

Book Design

Angela Saxon: whose work and ideas are hip, upbeat, and brilliant.

Editing and Proofreading

Melinda Mathias-Porter: whose wordsmithing was good fortune for the book.

Grace Truax: who, as copy editor, made everything better with the greatest of ease.

Illustration

Glenn Wolff: who fearlessly rendered my inner and outer life in breathtaking images.

Spiritual Sustenance

The teachers, saints, sages, and scholars who taught me to look in interesting and unanticipated places for that which I was seeking.

John and Angela Pate: whose friendship sustained me during the many months of writing in Florida.

Rob and Val Earle: whose generosity taught me why New Zealand is such an amazing country (endless ribbing for my $150.00 NZD traffic ticket for running a yellow light in downtown Nelson notwithstanding.)

Cherry Earle: A wise woman whose poems paint the universal experience.

Animals At My Side

My dog, Ollie: who reminded me that I could be just as creative running (him) on the beach as in front of a computer. Love on four legs.

My horses, Nell and Petie: when I needed to remember what is true and good, I would walk out to the pasture and put my hands on them. Then, and only then, could I return to the writing.

My goats, Thumper and Luna: who returned my sense of humor to me whenever it went missing. That's right, goats telling the Capricorn what's funny.

My cat, Mouse: who asked nothing of me, but gave her loving presence in the office and orchard while I wrote.

How To Use This Guide

This book is written for everyone in midlife and beyond. It is also written to give those individuals born between 1936 and 1979 a closer look, because they are approaching, in, or past midlife at the time of publishing. I will, in the near future, add a new set of Travel Groups for those born after 1979 to coincide with their midlife journey.

If you were born between 1936 and 1979, or know someone who was, this book can provide insight into the most important stage of life. Whether it's obtaining 20/20 vision on a time past, preparing for midlife to come, or navigating your journey in the present, *A Guide for Midlife* will help you see your life in a completely different light.

There is no best way to read this book, but there is a way to get the best out of it. To get properly oriented, follow the steps on the following pages.

1. Locate your Travel Group

There are four Travel Groups: North, South, East, and West, each comprised of a ten-year span of birth years. Find your birth year from among these groups to determine your placement:

🧳	North Travel Group	Born 1936-1946
🧳	South Travel Group	Born 1947-1957
🧳	East Travel Group	Born 1958-1968
🧳	West Travel Group	Born 1969-1979

You have millions of companions! Every person in the world that was born in your birth year is a member of your Travel Group.

2. Identify the Order of your Crises and Your Age at Each Crisis

In the table below, the order of crises for your Travel Group is the order in which your midlife crises occur. You can read the book chapters accordingly to get a sense of your unfolding path through midlife. Also find in the table below your approximate age at each of your six crises.

💼 North Travel Group: Born 1936-1946

Order of Crises	Approximate Age at Crisis
Second Call	37
Crisis of Authenticity	39-40
Crisis of Clarity	41
Crisis of Stature	42-44
Crisis of Power	46-41
Crisis of Balance and Beliefs	48
Crisis of Contribution	50

💼 South Travel Group: Born 1947-1957

Order of Crises	Approximate Age at Crisis
Crisis of Power	40-37
Second Call	37
Crisis of Authenticity	40-39
Crisis of Clarity	41
Crisis of Stature	45-43
Crisis of Balance and Beliefs	48
Crisis of Contribution	50

💼 East Travel Group: Born 1958-1968

ORDER OF CRISES	APPROXIMATE AGE AT CRISIS
Crisis of Power	37-36
Second Call	37
Crisis of Clarity	40-41
Crisis of Authenticity	39-42
Crisis of Stature	44-42
Crisis of Balance and Beliefs	48
Crisis of Contribution	50

💼 West Travel Group: Born 1969-1979

ORDER OF CRISES	APPROXIMATE AGE AT CRISIS
Crisis of Power	36-37
Second Call	37
Crisis of Clarity	40
Crisis of Authenticity	42-44
Crisis of Stature	42-45
Crisis of Balance and Beliefs	48
Crisis of Contribution	50

Note: For an ascending age range for a given crisis (for example, 42-44) those born in the first third of the birth-year span will be approximately 42, while those born in the middle years of the birth year span will be approximately 43, and those born in the last third of the birth year span will be approximately 44 at that crisis. For a descending age range for a given crisis (for example, 46-41) the same method applies as above.

These are the best age approximations I can give (using these charts). Given the complexity of the calculations required, if you wish to obtain more exact information, please refer to the Traveler's FAQ's section at the back of this book.

Additional Notes

Some people will experience two crises at the same time, although not necessarily for the same length of time. You can determine which of your crises overlap from the table. In the case of overlapping crises, you will be able to recognize, from the information in the chapters, which of your life events belongs to which crisis, and be empowered to navigate each with the information given.

Life sometimes gives you hints about the nature of a coming crisis a few months before it begins. Maintain awareness.

Some issues that you may be experiencing during a crisis may not find final resolution until a few months after the end of the crisis. This is why many people wish to obtain the exact dates for each of their crises.

This is a Story Within a Story!

Now that you have identified your Travel Group, you can read each chapter in the order in which your crises occur. But wait! Having been born in 1952, I'm a member of the South Travel Group and have written this guide in the order that my crises occurred for a good reason: there is a compelling story that runs through my midlife, as may be the case for you. If you read McKenzie's Journals out of the chapter order given in the book, you'll miss out on the drama that unfolded as my midlife proceeded from crisis to crisis. Therefore, to get the full effect of what happened in my life, first read McKenzie's Journals in the order that they appear in the book. Then, go back and read the chapters in the order specific for your own Travel Group. Now you can journey once, twice, or many times through *A Guide for Midlife*. May both your reading and real-life sojourns be adventures!

THE SECOND CALL

At the Crossroads, Stop, Look, and Listen

With your first breath, your soul commits to its purpose.
In your first breath, Life proclaims its passion for that purpose,
and places your life map within you.

THE TERRITORY OF THE CALL

The feeling of strong attraction exerted by a particular way of life

YOUR APPROXIMATE AGE

North Travel Group (1936-1946)   37
SouthTravel Group   (1947-1957)   37
East Travel Group   (1958-1968)   37
West Travel Group   (1969-1979)   37

TIME IN TRANSIT

18.6 years

WHAT TO PACK OR ACQUIRE ALONG THE WAY

Physical: Attunement with your body
Mental: Curiosity
Emotional: Resilience
Spiritual: Openness

WHAT TO LEAVE BEHIND

Other's voices

THE WEATHER FORECAST

Sun and clouds

THE MANTRA

My heart knows my higher life purpose.

Travel Itinerary

Every 18.6 years during your lifetime, a universal alarm clock reminds you of your higher life purpose. What are you here to do? What are you here to be? Each of these "calls" offers an answer to these questions. If you are to take your life purpose to successively higher elevations of expression, then you will need to hear and heed each call at age 18, 37, 56, 74, and 93.

The Second Call, at age 37, is both an ending and a beginning. It represents the conclusion of some aspects of your life as it opens a door to a new place. This call, like the one that occurred when you were 18 or 19 years old, presents you with an opportunity to set in motion your True Doing and True Being. When these two are united, you become aligned with your higher life purpose.

What is your True Doing? The dynamic function that you have come into this world to carry out. Your True Doing can express itself through your vocation, avocation, or interests. As your life proceeds from call to call, the main theme of your True Doing can be expressed in a variety of ways. For example, a teacher can teach in a classroom setting during one part of life and then continue teaching by writing or consulting at a later stage. The theme of "teacher" remains the same, while the form of teaching may change. The True Doing can also be as subtle as simply being resourceful in whatever you do, irrespective of a specific vocation or avocation.

What is your True Being? The Creative Spirit containing infinite attributes. As you express your True Doing, the attributes needed for the fulfillment of your higher life purpose flow from your creative spirit. An individual's True Doing as a parent, for instance, might bring forth the attributes of patience, perseverance, and generosity. An individual's True Doing as an accountant might bring forth the attributes of discrimination and precision. You are not defined by what you do. Instead, you become what you are meant to be as you develop the attributes of your True Being through the action of your True Doing.

How do you come to know your True Doing and True Being? At each call, whether you are aware of them or not, both inner and outer signs are present in a perfect match with your genuine yearnings. If you are out of touch with your purpose, then you may have to look, listen, and feel—and follow the signs!

A Great Guide: The Higher Self

Your Higher Self resides in your heart. It is present in everyone and speaks in every language and through every culture. If you look and listen to it, you can perceive true guidance for your life. This guidance most often comes as a voice, a sense, or a feeling that is simple, clear, dignified, and direct. When you enlist your Higher Self, it can lead you to your higher life purpose and show you how to fulfill it. It can also guide you skillfully through each midlife challenge, present you with high-road choices that you may not have previously considered, and show you how to take action consistent with those choices.

UNIVERSAL THEMES

At the Second Call, everyone's experience is unique, but within each experience some universal themes can exist:

1. Discovering a path distinctly different from the one that you have been traveling.

You might be unconsciously living out the unfulfilled dreams of authority figures or caregivers from your childhood. You might be persuaded or coerced into carrying on certain traditions or roles when you are really meant to create new ones. Pressures to conform can come from familial, educational, social, religious, or cultural influences.

You may arrive at the Second Call having mistaken the path that outer influences point to for your true path. In fact, you may have been on a detour for so long that you have come to think of it as being your correct route!

Some detours can drown out the voice of your Higher Self—the part of you that knows your correct direction. Detours can also result in anxiety, resistance, ill health, depression, or melancholy. See these as an inner summons to find the source of your genius and bring it to life. If you are experiencing any of these difficulties at the Second Call, direct your attention into the darkness of your own interior where your higher life purpose and passion—your creative genius—is waiting for you. This inner inquiry is not self-absorption, but rather a focused attention on your deepest needs and desires. The spiritual light of the wealth that these challenges hold is directly proportional to the darkness of the depths you plumb to find it.

If you are tempted to feel that you've lost valuable time with respect to finding your purpose, remember that detours can many times lead you right to it. No matter where you are in life, your life purpose is always there, waiting for you to arrive.

In any case, the Second Call gives you an inner prompting to find the route to your True Doing. If your life path has been determined for you by past influences and indoctrinations that you do not believe are right for you, find the courage to break free. Authority figures of your past may still be alive and well, but ultimately the decision about the road you take is yours to make. The purpose that you carried into this world at your birth it is still there. Find it!

Sometimes it is difficult to see your path clearly at first. Remain open, observant, and flexible. If or when things seem difficult, do not despair: help often arrives at the intersection of surrender. Surrender is not a giving up but is an opening that occurs when you are willing to ask for direction. Engage your senses and look, listen, and feel both outwardly and inwardly. The signs will be everywhere.

> The only thing I have to declare is my genius.
> Oscar Wilde, to a New York airport customs agent

Your higher life purpose is calling you to a life filled with meaning. Test any new interest for its effect of filling your body with energy. Let go of that which does not stir your inner flame. You are looking for that which elicits your rapt curiosity, attention, and passionate interest.

There is no substitute for the reason you were born and only you can carry out your higher life purpose. If you have not discovered this purpose by the age of thirty-seven, the Second Call offers you another opportunity. This is the time to jettison what is not yours. When you are willing to create your path with your own steps, you are on the way to thriving for the rest of your life.

Traveling Companions

Michael, Ireland

Michael, an actor, grew up in a family where the sons were expected to work in the legal profession. Because "life as an actor" was not a part of the family tradition, Michael struggled against his family's expectations. The ghosts of his ancestors drew out his guilt through his nightly dreams.

The sound of Michael's First Call eventually grew louder than the voices of his father and his ancestors. At the age of nineteen, he left home to work in a musical troupe, which, at his Second Call, he expanded into a young actors guild that was acclaimed for its social messages of peace.

Hong Hoa Lam, Vietnam

At the age of thirty-three, Hong Hoa Lam moved from Viet Nam to the United States with her husband and her brother to begin a new life. When she was thirty-six, she expressed the desire to open a restaurant in their neighborhood. Both her husband and brother vehemently disapproved: they cited traditional Vietnamese expectations that she, as a woman and mother, should take care of the home and children. Hong Hoa relented—and dismissed her dream.

At her Third Call, at age fifty-six, she re-proposed the idea to her husband. With their children raised and on their own, he agreed. Hong

Hoa welcomes her patrons at her popular and flourishing restaurant every night with a light in her eyes that reflects her passion.

TANYA, GERMANY

During Tanya's undergraduate years, her mother had pressed her to study the sciences—a curriculum that she herself had yearned to study. The early death of Tanya's grandfather had rendered the family financially incapable of sending her mother to a university. Tanya put her love for dance aside and accepted the education that her mother so earnestly offered.

After graduation, Tanya began working as a research chemist—a position she held for thirteen years. During that time, she suffered from bouts of severe depression. A failed suicide attempt at the age of thirty-six prompted her to seek help. During a deep exploration of her life, Tanya discovered, much to her surprise, a passion for yoga. She left her job to become a yoga instructor, allowing her own true desire to replace her mother's well-intended but misdirected influence on her life.

Today, Tanya is widely respected by yoga and dance studios for her talents. Her depression no longer overshadows her life; instead, it keeps her focused on and faithful to her higher life purpose as a yoga instructor.

2. Continuing to expand the dream, interest, or vision that you had in childhood or during your First Call at age eighteen or nineteen.

Childhood daydreams or night dreams contain important clues about the reason you were born. These dreams are frequently symbolic and, with correct interpretation, can point you directly to your higher life purpose.

During your childhood, authority figures or caregivers may have honored your dreams and helped you to bring about your specific life purpose. These figures helped you to align with your higher life purpose.

If your life circumstances have supported your passion from or before the First Call, excellent! Here, at the Second Call, explore how you might expand it or express it differently.

Traveling Companions

Mother Teresa, India

At the age of twelve, Agnes Gonxha Bojaxhiu of Skopje, Macedonia, felt a strong pull towards becoming a missionary. At age eighteen, she answered her First Call by leaving her childhood home to join the Sisters of Loreto, an Irish community of nuns with missions in India. There, she taught geography and catechism at St. Mary's Bengali Medium School for Girls in Calcutta, India.

On September 10, 1946, she was traveling by train to Darjeeling to rest and recuperate from a bout with tuberculosis. It was on that day that she received "the call within the Call." Describing this as "God wanting something more" from her, she expanded her work as a teacher by creating an open-air school for children living in Calcutta slums. Having no funds to begin her project, she depended on divine providence and soon thereafter received a flow of volunteer and financial support that enabled her to extend the reach of her endeavors.

VAL, NEW ZEALAND

After graduating with a degree in education from Christchurch Teachers College, Val traveled to Vancouver, Canada, for her two-year overseas adventure. She stayed for thirty years, working as a teacher in the public school system. At age thirty-seven, Val established a groundbreaking program for children with disabilities. After developing the resources and curricula needed, she organized families, teachers, administrators, and the city government in integrating institutionalized children into the public school system.

"The idea of being able to facilitate understanding and a sense of community among both challenged and 'normal' children and adults gave me a solid sense of my place in the world," Val recalls. "As I look back, I see that this time was critical to my next work to follow—that of coordinating the program in one hundred and twenty schools throughout Vancouver over the next many years."

3. Re-considering your call.

Life can bring events or circumstances that do not necessarily fit with your idea of what your life purpose is supposed to be. At first glance, the Second Call may feel inconvenient, or worse, a burden. But remember, all paths are noble and your path is perfect for you even though it may not, at first glance, appear to be. In recognizing and embracing "what is" at the Second Call, you will discover what "can be." Prepare to be surprised at that which is mobilized from within you to bring the world what it needs, and can only get, from you.

TRAVELING COMPANIONS

DIANE, UNITED STATES

At age thirty-seven, Diane was diagnosed with stage-four breast cancer and given two years to live. Refusing to be viewed as a statistic, she set out to prove wrong the doctor's prognosis. In between countless radiation and chemotherapy treatments, she formed an organization in her community to support and educate women with newly diagnosed breast cancer. She believed that, with support and education, a woman could outlive medical establishment statistics. Diane's organization grew to over three hundred women volunteers, working to provide support and education to women newly diagnosed with breast cancer. Diane lived not for two years, but for twelve.

MICHAEL J. FOX, UNITED STATES

From the PBS Frontline episode about Parkinson's disease, "My Father, My Brother, and Me," Dave Iverson interviewed Michael J. Fox. Excerpts reprinted with permission.

DAVE IVERSON: But sometimes that unwanted wake up call arrives when you are young and your career is just taking off. Michael J. Fox kept his diagnosis secret for seven years, but at the age of thirty-seven he decided it was time to go public and bring new attention to the disease.

MICHAEL J. FOX: When you are faced with something real, it demands something of you that you wouldn't have chosen for yourself. This is a real opportunity to help people.

DI: The same month that Michael J. Fox went public, November 1998, Parkinson's was back in the headlines for a different reason. A startling scientific development—embryonic stem cells, cells that are derived from embryo rather than fetal tissue—opened a new door of possibility....Suddenly there was the promise of creating cells that could replace what goes wrong in any number of diseases, and Parkinson's was Exhibit A....In the fall of 1999, Senator Arlen Specter convened a hearing on Parkinson's.... The hearing inspired Fox to start his own foundation, which soon became the leading independent funder of Parkinson's research.

DI: ...So it goes back to what you were saying—you wouldn't go back to where you were before, pre-Parkinson's, because while you have a loss, you have that much more, and you're busy filling that gap.

MJF: It is a total privilege, without question. This Parkinson's, it's a fact of who I am; it's part of me, right now. This is my life and I wouldn't trade it for anything.

4. Acknowledging the potential of death.

If death comes at the Second Call, you will leave a legacy to the world. Every legacy has a purpose and a message. At the time of death, the light of your life's purpose is released into the world. Will you be living your higher life purpose at the moment of your death?

TRAVELING COMPANIONS

PRINCESS DIANA, GREAT BRITAIN

Diana, Princess of Wales, was killed in an automobile accident in Paris, France, on August 31, 1997. At thirty-six years of age, she died at the threshold of her Second Call. Diana left many gifts to the world, not the least of which was the True Being attribute of compassion.

The Second Call offers a more conscious relationship between you and the world. It is universally synchronized with the threshold of midlife for the opportunities that each midlife crisis holds. Discovery of and commitment to your higher life purpose is only the first choice of many that you will make over the next 18.6 years, as you make your way to the Third Call at age fifty-six and each Call beyond. Your higher life purpose and the world's need for it are a dovetail.

The Ultimate Travel Tip:

Slow, Caution, Yield, and Curve Ahead signs are posted for your safe passage. Proceed with self-determination and claim your joy!

McKenzie's Journal

December 23, 1988 • I am thirty-six today. I keep reminding myself that I live in Tokyo, Japan. How in the world did I get dropped into this city of fourteen million people halfway around the world from home?

Bill invites some of our expatriate friends to celebrate at my favorite restaurant in Shibuya. Expatriates are true adventurers. I've never regarded myself as one, but being with them makes me feel like I've joined a new tribe that I already know. How does that work?

April 9, 1989 • Bill and I are in Maui for corporate functions. I have two weeks to play, but play is not what I want to do right now. A short time ago I would have been shopping my head off and lying around the pool with the other corporate spouses. It suddenly bores me silly.

April 15, 1989 • We celebrate Bill's forty-eighth birthday tonight. He drinks way too much, once again, and I don't see how he can always get up the next day and function as well as he does.

April 16, 1989 • While Bill is in meetings, I look up my Aunt Pat who has lived on Maui since divorcing my uncle twelve years ago. As we sit on her deck overlooking the ocean, I can't believe how changed she is from the bejeweled, Chicago doctor's wife I once knew. Now her clothes are flowing and flowered, and her long hair is pulled back in a ponytail. Boy, is she ever a long way gone from those cardigans and coifs. She tells me about her life here. Bookshelves filled with books on spirituality, metaphysics, and mysticism. Where's my *Food and Wine* magazine?

While we eat lunch she speaks about universal cycles and patterns and how they reflect all events in life. She tells me that all we need to know is inside ourselves, and that life offers a constant stream of inner and outer messages that enable us to align with its natural flow. Even though I know that I've landed on another planet (her house) something urges me to accept her invitation to dinner tomorrow night. Assuredly, that will be without Bill. As I drive back to the hotel, I imagine how he'd react to all of this stuff. Not good.

April 19, 1989 • Tonight during dinner, Aunt Pat returns to yesterday's conversation, mostly about metaphysics. She gives me three books to take with me. When I get back to the hotel room, I hide them in the bottom of my suitcase. Bill would think I've lost my mind.

April 21, 1989 • We return to Tokyo. Takumi-san, our driver, is there to meet us. After Maui, Tokyo is gray and depressing. I hate it when traffic backs up in the tunnels because the exhaust fumes get into the Benz despite the air conditioning system. I just hold my breath for as long as I can.

April 22, 1989 • A rare quiet afternoon at the apartment. I open one of the books Aunt Pat gave me. I don't know how to say this any other way: even though I've never read this stuff before, everything in the book seems familiar to me! How can I recognize information I've not read nor heard of before? Stranger than that, it's unbelievably fascinating.

April 23, 1989 • I wake up to a dream this morning: I'm walking along a dusty road in a foreign country. A horse, unhaltered, walks ahead of me. It's leading me somewhere. I follow it without needing to know where it's going because I find the horse profoundly easy to trust. What a feeling, that kind of trust. The dream ends before I find out where the horse is leading me.

April 25, 1989 • Despite the hectic schedule this week, I start another of Aunt Pat's metaphysics books. The more I read, the more interested I become in this stuff…and the more different I feel from myself. It's like existing in two worlds, which is really confusing and downright scary.

July 2, 1989 • We're back in the States for a month of vacation. Since the Grand Rapids house is mothballed, we drive directly from the airport to the cabin. After twenty-two hours in transit, two hours is like two minutes. I cry like a baby when I see Ciao running down the road to us as we drive into Twin Lakes. I know it's best that she be here with Jim, the caretaker while we're in Japan, but it's really hard on me not to have my dog. I'm just grateful that she has woods and water to be herself in.

August 4, 1989 • I've done everything I've wanted to do in the last month: watch the loons raise their chicks; walk the woods and swim the lakes with Ciao; and fly-fish for rainbows with Bill (one of the best forms of intimacy.)

August 6, 1989 • Back in Japan, where the concrete of the Tokyo summer makes me feel like I'm living in a giant furnace. No time to complain, though, as I'm sweating full out on the squash court anyway. Insanely busy schedule of corporate functions. I love the Japanese people!

October 21, 1989 • My life is an outer whirlwind of new experiences and an inner whirlwind of confusion. My reading of metaphysics has become a full immersion study. I move between my living room/classroom, corporate functions, and Tokyo American Club activities. My life is not dull, but my life also seems like movement in two different directions at the same time. Is this actually possible?

December 17, 1989 • Bill and I are skiing in Santa Fe and Taos, New Mexico. This area of the country is so different, and so interesting. We stay at a Taos inn and Bill likes the log furniture so much that he orders several pieces to be made for the cabin. Cool!

December 23, 1989 • Onward from Santa Fe to the cabin and my doggie.

December 24, 1989 • We celebrated my thirty-seventh birthday last night with some friends who are also at their cabins for the holidays. Bill gives me a beautiful art print of a loon. My love of loons has grown into an obsession.

January 1, 1990 • Happy New Year! The snow is pristine, the deer and wild turkeys are visible in the woods, and my dog never leaves my side. I snowshoe while Bill ice fishes with his buddies.

January 4, 1990 • Return to Tokyo. No snow, can't see the moon.

February 2, 1990 • Corporate functions, platform tennis, squash, calligraphy, and Ikebana lessons at the Tokyo American Club with the other spouses. My world has become wide with travel to South Korea, Thailand, Singapore, Hong Kong, Australia, and many European countries. I am high on the sights, sounds, and smells of it all.

March 6, 1990 • I'm having countless and wonderful experiences in this amazing country. As the company president's wife, I am living the first-class life of a princess. But as full with new experiences, I'm also suddenly feeling empty. I want to go back to the cabin. I want to go home.

March 9, 1990 • I wander up and down the streets of Tokyo again today. It's been my pass-the-time thing for about six months. Today I realize that I'm not wandering. I am totally lost.

March 10, 1990 • I miss Ciao. Choosing a Labrador retriever was the best thing I could have chosen for cabin life, but she's there and I'm here. I miss my friends and my life in the States. What is my life supposed to be in a foreign country three thousand miles from home? It's well and fine for Bill: his life is so nicely defined by his position of turning around a failing company. By agreeing to come here I've yanked apart all the threads of my life. The expatriate "honeymoon" is over. I'm suddenly at the bottom of a deep, dark well.

March 12, 1990 • I have a difficult time getting to sleep. It feels darker inside me than it is in this bedroom. At 4 A.M. I hear a voice. It's not my voice. It's…foreign. It's down here in the bottom of the well with me, advising me to surrender. Surrender? Surrender to what? To whom?

March 13, 1990 • The same voice again. It tells me that right now my assignment is to "not know." It's scary for me to not know—my father used to beat me when I didn't know.

April 30, 1990 • My confusion about my life keeps an unyielding grip on me. I have to talk to Bill, but when and how do I share all of this craziness without seeming crazy? Maybe I really am crazy.

May 1, 1990 • I finish reading a book about an indigenous method of accessing higher realms of the mind that exist beyond the brain. This "mind" contains all knowledge, freely accessed by anyone. My University of Illinois Bachelor of Science degree doesn't know what to do with this. Confusion wrestles with an unexpected, voracious hunger for more. One of the books mentions the Light Institute in Santa Fe, New Mexico, where this kind of process is practiced. What if I…? Forget it, Bill would freak out.

May 3, 1990 • Bill and I have breakfast together at the New Otani Hotel. Over my plate of French toast, I unload my angst about what I'm supposed to be doing with my life. I tell him what I'm reading. As I listen to myself, I sound like someone else. He puts his head down. This is the last thing he wants to hear. He tells me he never had this problem when he was my age. What was wrong with what "we" were doing here in Tokyo, he wants to know? He reminds me that I'm his wife and "isn't that enough?" Makes me doubt myself—really doubt myself. How was I supposed to know that this was going to happen?

May 4, 1990 • I tell Bill that I want to go home to the cabin. I have always been known for my incessant talking, but now I need to listen and the cabin is the only place where I can do

> I can never be what I ought to be until you are what you ought to be. You can never be what you ought to be until I am what I ought to be. This is the way the world is made.
> Dr. Martin Luther King, Jr.

that. He's unhappy with my decision. I feel like I'm abandoning him by leaving for a while, but I feel like I'll die if I don't get home.

May 7, 1990 • The twenty-two hours of travel are worth it. My beautiful dog and I are together again. How I have missed her. Her life here at the Club with Jim, the caretaker, is best for her for right now, I guess. She's able to run in the woods and swim in the lakes like she was born to do. I want to be her.

Ciao and I walk the woods and kayak the lakes at all times of day and night. The loons call at 3 A.M. Their wails pull at something inside of me.

May 8, 1990 • Ciao lies at my feet on the dock while I sip coffee. We watch the mist unfurl and spiral upwards from the surface of the lake.

I call the Light Institute in Santa Fe this afternoon. I don't even know the questions to ask, but I make an appointment anyway. Have I just jumped off the dock…or a cliff?

May 15, 1990 • Bill and I talk on the phone today. I can tell he's lonely because I hear the sound of alcohol in his voice. It's not easy being apart, but it's also difficult for me to be there when I need so badly to be with myself.

May 21, 1990 • I finish the two books of required reading for my appointment at the Light Institute. Higher Self…Higher Mind…what in the world am I getting myself into? And I thought Japan was a foreign country!

May 29, 1990 • I finally tell Bill that I'm going to New Mexico. To my surprise, he's not surprised. He cuts me off when I try to explain. It's real clear that I'm on my own with this one.

It's not what you are,
it's what you don't
become that hurts.

Oscar Levant

June 8, 1990 • At the Albuquerque airport, I rent a car and follow Interstate 25 North as it winds through the desert toward Santa Fe. Halfway there, tears come out of nowhere. They feel like the ones I cry when I come home to the cabin from Japan. Oh my God, the sights and sounds in the Plaza make me feel like a piece of white bread that wishes it were whole wheat.

June 9, 1990 • The map to the Light Institute directs me down a long, dusty road into a small village outside of Santa Fe. Horses are grazing in a pasture by the entrance gate. I recall the dream I had at the cabin about an unbridled horse leading me down a dusty road. My God, the horse in the dream is right here, right now. Is this where it was leading me?

Today, my first session with my Higher Self shows me myself as a two-year-old toddler. In her, I re-experience the precious qualities that I once had but seemed to have lost along the way to adulthood. It was wordlessly wonderful to once again be myself as this child…to see how perfect she is just as she is, and to see how she accepts herself without question as this perfection. In the closing moment of the session, my facilitator prompts me to ask the child what she wishes to give me: she gives me the gift of freedom. I thought I knew what freedom felt like—until this moment.

June 10, 1990 • During my second session, I meet another "me" who lives within. The other me is not just love, but limitless love. How have I lived for so long without knowing of this limitlessness? I've been living, but have I really been alive? I'm alive, but have I really been living?

June 11, 1990 • Third session today. What word describes the bodily sensation of truth? I'm the one who wanted to know, and it seems that my curiosity has led me straight to it—by way of my body. All my life, I assumed I was in my body—until today.

June 12, 1990 • My fourth and last session today. My Higher Self shows me my life purpose, but it is encoded within symbolism that, as Blaire tells me, will reveal itself over time. "Meaning" is what I'm after. What is the meaning of my life? My life will mean something when I live my life purpose. This is typical of me to state the obvious but really, how can it be any other way?

> The new earth arises as more and more people discover that their main purpose in life is to bring the light of consciousness into this world and to use whatever they do as a vehicle for consciousness.
>
> Eckhart Tolle

> The mountaintop experience of God is within you—and it waits for you to call it forth. The Hebrews called this inner power El Shaddai, the mountaintop experience, who created you and dwells within you. From that high and lofty place of being, you can see exactly what is yours to do and how to do it. How can you get in touch with your higher power, the intuitive self—that part of you that can create a life of peak performance and expression? Simply call it forth and it will come forth!
>
> Greg Barrette

June 13, 1990 • Back to Michigan and Ciao. I kayak across the lake to see the loons while Ciao swims off the bow. Through binoculars, I watch the parents-to-be taking turns incubating the two tan, speckled eggs on their nest. I feel like one of those eggs.

June 14, 1990 • I let Bill convince me to return to Japan a few days earlier than scheduled. Why am I nervous? I have to say good-bye to Ciao again. How many more times? I remember when Bill named her Ciao, Italian for "hello" and "good-bye." It seems to have been prophetic because constant hellos and good-byes now define our relationship.

June 25, 1990 • Takumi-san, our driver, picks me up at Narita. Everything looks different: I can see into things. I can see into Takumi-san's heart. It's so good, so sweet. Through my sessions, I know the goodness and sweetness of my own heart; that's why I can recognize the same in his.

Bill calls on the car phone from the office. I've missed him. He's really happy that I'm back. How I love him. But, he's still mystified (putting it nicely) at what I'm doing, and barely tolerating my new "activities," as he calls them. This love is complicated.

Takumi-san drives Bill and me to Sabatini's in the Ginza for dinner. As usual, the conversation revolves around the corporation. I can only half listen to him as my heart clenches inside my chest. It's only half here.

July 2, 1990 • During my walks through the neighborhoods near Roppongi, I have discovered some Buddhist temples and Shinto shrines. Modern buildings rise and fall overnight, but these ancient places seem built to be eternal.

I watch Japanese people from all walks of life come to pray in the temples for better jobs, more money, good health, a husband or a wife. A calligrapher writes their prayers on small pieces of white paper that the visitors tie onto branches of trees and bushes outside.

Once in a while I happen upon a Shinto shrine that is empty of visitors, and that is the case today. The pristine courtyard footing of white gravel crunches loudly under my feet and makes me feel conspicuous. I sit alone on a small bench and watch the priests move in cadence with their daily tasks. I wonder if they are passionate about being priests.

It occurs to me how I have just drifted along through life, letting things happen to me. It seems like I've been following my life instead of leading my life. What a scary thought. During my sessions at the Light Institute, I learned how to actually ask inwardly for what I want. I never even knew I had an "inwardly" to ask!

July 5, 1990 • Jim calls from the cabin to let Bill and me know that two loon chicks hatched successfully yesterday. He tells us that Ciao is well. Hearing this makes me well.

July 29, 1990 • Bill climbs to the summit of Mt. Fuji for the second time. I think that his life here is about being at the summit of his work. He has re-architected the company, steering it out of a near financial crash to annual sales nearing one billion dollars annually. Since being on television and in the newspapers, people approach him (even in restaurants) for autographs! It's so cool to watch him.

> I always wanted to be somebody, but I should have been more specific.
>
> Lily Tomlin

August 5, 1990 • The stifling heat and humidity are made worse by today's rain. Soot collects on the patio furniture. I can't fathom the fact that this stuff is collecting in my lungs. I sequester myself in the apartment all day, reading the books that Diane has sent me from the States. She and I talk on the phone once a week. Her fight with breast cancer is a study in staunch courage. What must it be like to be diagnosed with stage-four breast cancer at the age of thirty-seven?

September 10, 1990 • Today I'm at another Buddhist temple. There's no one around except for the calligrapher so it's very quiet. My relationship with silence is sort of like a forbidden relationship with a mysterious, but compelling stranger: I long for it, but don't know how to approach it. As for the calligrapher, he intrigues me. He seems at such peace with his pen.

On the way back to the apartment, I notice the Franciscan Chapel in Roppongi. How many times have I passed by it but not seen it until now? Something makes me stop and park on the street outside. It's been a long time since I've been in a Catholic church….

I remember my teenage misdemeanors in Catholic school, like rolling my uniform skirt up at the waistband to hike the hem above my knees, defying the nuns, and serving communion to my friends in the chapel when the sisters went to cloister after classes. I delighted in Catholic disobedience.

At the far end of the vestibule of the Chapel is a bulletin board with a sign asking for volunteers to make rice cakes for the homeless. I've never volunteered for anything in my life. (Well, I volunteered to come here for Bill, but that's different.) Standing here in the Chapel, reading the notice, a compelling need to help the homeless washes over me. I don't know why.

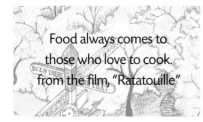

Food always comes to those who love to cook.
from the film, "Ratatouille"

September 13, 1990 • I begin my volunteer job at the Franciscan Chapel. In the basement kitchen, I prepare rice in a big cooker, let it cool, and then form handfuls of it into small triangular cakes, topping each with a tiny pickled plum. Other volunteers pick up the cakes and deliver them to the homeless, who sleep in Tokyo's train stations.

I miss Ciao today and feel sad that I am not home with her. I feel as homeless as the homeless I'm making rice cakes for.

September 27, 1990 • This morning at the Chapel, Father mentions that a Catholic priest from India will be visiting for a couple of weeks. When I hear this, something strange happens: my body heats up like a furnace. I ask for an appointment with him. I don't know why I ask. I am both surprised and terrified at this, my own request. Am I nuts?

October 9, 1990 • Early this morning, before preparing the rice cakes, I hear the Indian priest moving around in his room next to the kitchen. I break into a cold sweat while waiting for him in the all-purpose room. When we finally sit down together, I hear myself tell him that I am searching, but I don't know for what. He gently reaches over and touches my forehead. The next thing I know I am flat on the floor, unable to speak.

> The Voice of the Holy Spirit does not command, because it is incapable of arrogance. It does not demand, because it does not seek control. It does not overcome, because it does not attack. It merely reminds. It is compelling only because of what it reminds you of.
> from "A Course In Miracles"
> (r) T-5.II.7:1-5

I don't remember driving back to the apartment. I say nothing to Bill about this. The lines between us are unsteady enough as it is these days. I don't need to be falling off the high wire right now.

December 8, 1990 • It's Diane's forty-third birthday today. I call her on the phone. She tells me that the cancer has moved into her spine and that she has to begin another round of chemotherapy. Chemo, chemo, chemo, and tons of radiation are what her life has been for six years now.

Throughout all of this, though, she continues to give talks to various community groups about her journey, while living under the weight of uncertainty. And she still finds room to counsel me on what life direction I might take. Social work is one such suggestion that had not occurred to me. When we get off the phone, I cry and cry.

December 23, 1990 • Today is my thirty-ninth birthday. Dinner in the Ginza with friends. Expatriates are a very fun bunch!

February 28, 1991 • Time is accelerating. I'm swept along by countless corporate activities. Bill has opened the door to the world for me with the travel for his job. I tour the sights while he works in the various affiliate offices in Asia. Now in Bangkok, I visit shrines and temples, take a river cruise, and walk through markets and neighborhoods.

I observe people who seem to be content with much, much less than I. How much happier could I be with the knowledge of who I am, versus what I have? Being Bill's wife isn't who I am (even if I don't know who I am.) I just know that I have to stop defining my life through his!

April 15, 1991 • We celebrate Bill's fiftieth birthday tonight with expatriate and corporate friends. They love him. And so, so, so, do I.

June 15, 1991 • I am denied acceptance to the School of Social Work at Grand Valley State University. Now I'm even more confused. Where do I go now? What in the world am I supposed to do with my life? Am I already doing what I should be doing? Why can't I just be satisfied with who I am and what I have? (Uh oh, does this sound like my mother?)

September 11, 1991 • The Tokyo summer has been hot and humid. The endless concrete of this city is not for me. I miss being able to see the moon. I miss walking barefoot on the path around the lake at the cabin in the pitch dark, naming the night critters that I hear moving in the woods. I miss my dog. The loons are calling to me from three thousand miles away. It's time to go home—again.

Bill hates that I'm not totally here for him; I hate myself for not being here for him. But whatever is pulling me to the cabin is immense. As Bill's career demands grow, so do my heart demands. My flight to the cabin feels urgent. I struggle with guilt for leaving him and he barely stuffs his anger for being left. But, in the same way that he's on his career quest, I'm on my soul quest. And that quest feels stronger than both of us.

September 16, 1991 • I am at the cabin with Ciao! I walk, kayak, and swim, listen to the loons, watch the moon rise over the lake, and pick wild mushrooms for dinner. Nighttime scents from the woods drift over Ciao and me as we sleep crossways on the bed to catch moonbeams through the skylight. I'm never lonely here.

September 22, 1991 • I drive down to Grand Rapids to visit Diane. She's in bed. She wants to talk about regular life instead of hospital and cancer life. My life does not feel like a regular life. I drive to Arnie's Delicatessen to buy her a piece of chocolate cake. When I return she's too sick to eat it. Her sweet husband, Jim comes home from work and hangs out with us for a while and then leaves to play squash. Diane tells me about an idea that she has: she wants to create an organization to provide liaison assistance and education to women newly diagnosed with breast cancer. I take some notes to help her organize it.

September 26, 1991 • At the bookstore I discover books about transpersonal psychology. It strikes a chord. The premise is much like what I experienced in Santa Fe. It says that we are already whole, but must gather the fragmented parts of our personalities into an integrated state. Going beyond the personal, or the ego's, viewpoint, thus the word transpersonal, can do this.

September 30, 1991 • I'm going to call the Institute of Transpersonal Psychology in California to see if I can take external coursework.

October 1, 1991 • It's back to Japan. I return Ciao to the caretaker and drive away from the cabin—again. Her eyes plead for me to come back. It breaks my heart. What must being left behind be like for her? Twenty-two hours in transit from Detroit to Tokyo. It's a long haul going west, and as I turn my thoughts to Bill, I realize just how much I have missed him.

November 2, 1991 • A group of distributors has requested that I make an appearance at a rally at Hibiya Public Hall. I arrive only to discover that they expect me to make a twenty-minute speech! What am I going to say to two thousand Japanese women? With no prepared speech and my heart in my throat, there is only one thing I can do—let my heart do the talking. What comes out is: follow your heart. Despite the fact that this message is a little risky for the Japanese culture, the women's response is overwhelming. What a learning curve I'm on.

November 9–10, 1991 • This weekend I speak to three groups of eight thousand people each at Nihon Hall in Tokyo. The word is out among the distributors—my love for the Japanese people is reflected by their response to me. Bill really loves me doing this and will make arrangements for me to go anywhere in the country I am asked to speak.

December 20, 1991 • All of a sudden, I have a "job." In the last few weeks I have traveled to several cities in Japan, challenging the audiences (of up to fourteen thousand people!) to live their dream—while I'm still trying to find mine. Does that make me a fraud? I think it makes me one of them.

I have a purpose here today. It is a purpose I have tried to serve for many years. I have prayed that God would show me a way to accomplish it.

Al Gore, on the acceptance of the Nobel Peace Prize, December 10, 2007, Oslo, Norway

Sherpa Norbu's Parable

I am Norbu, member of a long lineage of Sherpa. We have lived at the foot of the mountain for longer than any anyone can remember. Today, I will lead the way up the mountain, as I have done countless times since my thirty-seventh year.

I gather with the climbers and porters at base camp. Juniper boughs burn on the rock altar, sending smoke skyward. As the wind snaps prayer flags back and forth to send their prayers of compassion into the world, the local priest performs a sacred ceremony for a safe passage to the summit. He blesses everyone, along with their climbing gear, and offers sungdhis, knotted strings, to wear around their necks for protection. At the conclusion of the ceremony, rice is thrown onto the altar as an offering to the gods for a safe passage.

After the first day's climb, I notice Shaypa sitting at the fire with her fellow porters. Although they talk and laugh together like a clan, she seems distracted. Being with them gives her a feeling of safety and a sense of belonging—but I sense that she is slightly uncomfortable.

The climbers sit apart from the porters at their own fire. As their guide, I know exactly how to get to the summit. Everyone is deeply connected to me. Some are not aware of this connection and therefore live in fear—and fear adds unnecessary weight to their backpacks. Those who are aware know that their bid for the summit is tenuous without a conscious connection to me. I trek toward the summit knowing all of this.

I know where I stand in relationship to the mountain. My steps are solid with experience. It is my responsibility to maintain balance at all times.

I have no attachment to the outcome of the climbers' and porters' treks. I do not carry anyone else's gear. I concern myself only with my relationship with the mountain. If that relationship is right, then all will be right.

I know that Shaypa is preparing to take responsibility for her life. I sense that she secretly wishes to obtain my counsel—but she is not divulging her wishes to the other porters because she fears that they may reject her. She may bear great hesitation, but the fire in her heart will, in time, burn away anything that holds her back.

So for now, Shaypa keeps her aspirations to herself. She does what she needs to do until the time is right. For a time, she will have to live in two worlds—as both porter and secret apprentice—while my steps teach hers. It is good training, because the mountain demands both perseverance and flexibility.

At the end of the day's climb, Shaypa and the other porters establish camp. My yurt is already set up. Although I seem to disappear into it I really do not. The climbers and porters don't know that I am always among them. In truth, I am everywhere on this mountain.

When the others are asleep, Shaypa comes to my yurt and whispers a request to enter. I direct her to place her boots next to mine outside the door and beckon her to sit across the fire from me. She doesn't know why I do not look directly at her. It is not necessary, for I see her clearly within myself. Someday she will understand this. I wait for her to speak.

"I want to become a Sherpa. I want to lead climbers to the summit. I want to know the mountain as you know it, to walk it as you walk it. But I am afraid to leave the safety of my fellow porters because they are all I have ever known."

I rise and go to my altar on the wall opposite the door. Shaypa's birth map, rolled and tied carefully with slender strands of hair from a horse's mane, lies among those of the other members of the climbing group. I lift it reverently and carry it back to my sitting place at the fire. I unfurl it carefully and study one particular glyph among the many that are also scribed upon it. This symbol is as old as the moon itself and its particular position on the map reflects her sense of urgency.

"Your timing is perfect!" I exclaim.

Shaypa's eyes widen with surprise and expectation.

"If you want to be a Sherpa," I tell her, pointing to the map, "you will have to let go of your small world to gain an infinite one. You will have to give up the safety that you believe your clan gives you to gain the true sanctuary of your Self. You will have to relinquish what you believe to be true about yourself for that which is actually true. You will have to cease serving fear in order to serve your purpose. You have a dawning awareness of another you. This 'other you' knows itself like I know the mountain. You have arrived here in perfect timing to take responsibility for your higher life purpose."

"You are leaving old ways behind for higher elevations," I continue. "Let go of what or where you think the path should be and take only the path that is lit by the light in your heart."

I tell her, "Few in this world know that my true purpose is worth giving up everything for. Every step on the path connects me to gifts that are placed there just for me. In my every step is the joy of my True Doing and True Being. This is what I live for; this is why there is so much life in me."

"So you see," I assure her gently, "with such a life you really don't give up anything after all."

Shaypa understands everything I tell her. More importantly, she can feel the truth of it in her body. In remembering herself by recognizing herself in me, her choice is made easy.

Suddenly, our spirits rise, merging over the fire. As the flames settle back into a soft glow, I, Norbu Sherpa, am gone. The exchange has been made. Shaypa has chosen.

Alone before the dwindling fire, Shaypa watches the shadows of her former self fade. She patiently waits until just before dawn to emerge from the yurt. Everyone in the camp is still asleep. As she burns juniper, some of the climbers and porters awaken. Others do not.

Those who do awaken begin their preparations for the next phase of the ascent. It is still dark as they set off from camp. The climbers follow Shaypa without noticing any difference. Things continue just as before, but it is now she who is guiding them upward to the summit.

Shaypa is now a Sherpa. She is the first one up the path and the first to witness the dawning sun. It illuminates Shaypa with its brilliance, changing her forever.

Appearing on the path, I pluck a six-pointed star from the heavens and offer it to her. Holding it in her hands, it becomes a simple piece of bread. As she eats it, six attributes of her True Being come forth: Courage, Determination, Devotion, Strength, Enthusiasm, and Focus.

An eagle appears overhead. Opening its wings, it invites Shaypa into the empty space beneath them. As they fly together Shaypa can see a wider horizon. She can see as the eagle sees. All who abide under the eagle's wings are able to see the true nature of things. In this space, Shaypa is reunited with the reason for her birth. In the protective space under the eagle's wings, Shaypa realizes, with tears of joy, that she is home.

The eagle sets Shaypa safely back onto the path. It knows that she must walk every step of her life in order to embody the vision that it has given to her.

And now I, Norbu Sherpa, rise upward as the eagle. Circling overhead for a brief moment, I watch Shaypa Sherpa faithfully put one step in front of the other, her eyes oriented upward toward the summit. Her heart is open to herself and therefore to life.

The climbers think that they are following her physical presence, but Shaypa knows otherwise: she knows that Spirit lives in the empty space around her, just as the eagle showed her. It is in this empty space that anyone can remember who he or she really is, and for what purpose they ascend the mountain. In this space, everyone's Sherpa-Self sings him or her toward their summits.

What Other Me?

I long to see
the flight of wild geese
winging their way south.
In that still time of silence,
when the day looks backward
at the night,
a memory stirs in me
in some strange way
of blizzards howling from the north.

Where no geese fly has been my life,
where no blizzards blow,
and yet I seem to know!

What other me
can hear the wild geese
in their flight,
and thrill
to the certainty of their knowing,
the sure long-necked arrow
of their going?

What other me,
immersed in wind-blown snow,
remembers the clear day
of their passing
in the still night
when their honking filled the sky,
high and clear overhead
like a long, lonely cry?
What other me?

CHERRY EARLE, NEW ZEALAND

CRISIS OF AUTHENTICITY

Where Vision and Action become One

THE TERRITORY

The genuineness or truth of something

YOUR APPROXIMATE AGE

North Travel Group	(1936-1946)	39-40
South Travel Group	(1947-1957)	40-39
East Travel Group	(1958-1968)	39-41
West Travel Group	(1969-1979)	41-44

TIME IN TRANSIT

Up to 18 months

WHAT TO PACK OR ACQUIRE ALONG THE WAY

Physical:	Grounding
Mental:	Flexibility
Emotional:	Calm
Spiritual:	Self-trust

WHAT TO LEAVE BEHIND

That which is not yours

THE WEATHER FORECAST

Electrical storms

THE MANTRA

Expect the unexpected.

TRAVEL ITINERARY

Living authentically means living from the inside out. The purpose of the Crisis of Authenticity is to enable you to create a meaningful life by taking action on your vision.

This crisis awakens you to the authentic expression of your higher life purpose. It frees you of responsibilities that are inappropriate to your vision or that you may cling to through a misplaced sense of responsibility or false dutifulness.

Take a moment and consider:

> *Is what you are doing bringing you happiness?*
> *Do your family and friends support you in what you want to do?*
> *Have you been living your life solely to please others?*
> *Do you allow yourself to do that which makes you happy?*

On this part of the journey, respond to the call of freedom from within you. Make changes to liberate yourself from outworn ways of life. By suppressing your need for freedom at this time, the energy that is meant for your vision might be misspent in mindless and misappropriated rebellion, accidents, and unnecessary turmoil.

The Crisis of Authenticity brings about an awakening that can come as suddenly and unpredictably as lightning. In fact, at this time you are much like a lightning rod receiving a very high voltage of electricity. It is essential to direct the "current" constructively; otherwise, it will scatter and be wasted.

Once you are awake, you will need courage to activate the unique vision that lies within your heart. If you were not able to grasp the true purpose of your life at the Second Call, this may be a confusing time. But it is important to understand that radical redirection may be needed to reorient you toward the life you are meant to be living. Resistance to making necessary changes invites the possibility of chaos and turbulence. Recognize and acknowledge the wisdom behind any changes occurring now. If you are one who embraces change as a life "upgrade," you will find renewed vitality in a meaningful and creative life that reflects your truth.

Understand, too, that this is a critical point in your life journey. You may have fallen into deep ruts—and powerful universal forces are at work to free you from those ruts. Many individuals choose to continue to live in the past. They deny that new life is being offered, retreat into old patterns and call their life "good enough." Having squandered the precious resurgence of energy that this crisis gives, these individuals can experience a downward spiral into meaninglessness.

There are also potential pitfalls at this juncture. The first is allowing inflexibility and resistance to change to keep you stuck in the past. This can lead to a sense of inertia from which it may be difficult to recover. The second is acting too hastily. Move forward when you are in balance. The third is impulsively discarding your existing support systems. Balance your need for freedom with your responsibilities to the important parts of your life. Otherwise, they may not be there when this crisis has passed.

The Crisis of Authenticity can be characterized by sudden change, anxiety, restlessness, and confusion. Experimentation, resistance, rebellion, and inner and outer questioning are also aspects of this crisis. Separation from jobs, relationships, or prior interests may mark this time to indicate that redirection is needed. If you are experiencing depression, then it may be that you have yet to make the connection to your higher life purpose and the passion that resides within it. Brilliant ideas leading to new discoveries and inventions are often made during this period. Act on yours and share them with the world.

This time brings a resurgence of life force energy. Use this energy efficiently by focusing it on that which is important to you. Much like an electrical cord plugged into the socket to activate an appliance, you are now plugged into a higher-voltage universal life force energy to activate your vision. If you are so inclined, you can make conscious contact with your Higher Self and form a relationship with it through inner practices such as meditation or transpersonal states of consciousness; then allow it to guide you through this important time.

Will you sacrifice your life at the altar of unconscious conformity or celebrate life with your unmistakeable authenticity?

ESSENTIAL TRAVEL TIPS

- Express your vision. Speak with your true voice, the one that can only be heard when you have consciously become aware of the voices from your past that might still be directing your life.

- Find silence through solitude, meditation, or other means by which you can get to know the sound of your true voice.

- Lighten your load by releasing childhood conditioning and false conformity to the truths of others.

- Find the freedom to explore, experiment with, and convey your vision, but balance that with your existing responsibilities.

- Understand the difference between false dutifulness and correct responsibility.

- Learn how to differentiate between appropriate and inappropriate expectations and demands. Respectively, they will energize or deplete you.

- Accept changes now occurring in your life; they exist for the purpose of directing your life force energy into your vision-in-action.

- Choose constructive ways to stay grounded. Time spent in nature, exercise, and whole foods can stabilize and direct the high-voltage life force energy that is now flowing through you for the purpose of this crisis—finding and expressing your authenticity.

The Ultimate Travel Tip:

A change in direction does not mean a U-turn.

SIGHTS AND SOUNDS

This is a list of just some of the things that you will find along your way through the Crisis of Authenticity. You can recognize them as personal traits or as symbolic messages in your dreams. You are free to choose which of these can be of real and lasting assistance for the rest of your journey.

Abruptness	Bachelors	Eccentricity	Infidelity
Accidents	Bicycles	Electricity	Insight
Adultery	Catastrophe	Engineers	Innovation
Advancement	Change	Estrangement	Intellect
Airplanes	Clairvoyance	Flying	Intuition
Alienation	Contradiction	Freedom	Metaphysics
Altruism	Crisis	Genius	Miscarriage
Anarchy	Curiosity	Helicopters	Occultism
Animation	Desertion	Highways	Panic
Anxiety	Detachment	Homosexuality	Quests
Assertiveness	Detours	Humanitarians	Radicals
Astonishment	Disagreements	Iconoclasts	Railroads
Astrologers	Discovery	Ideas	Rebellion
Audacity	Disorganization	Idiosyncrasy	Rejection
Auras	Disruption	Impulsiveness	Resistance
Automobiles	Divorce	Independence	

Traveling Companions

Avery, United States

Avery, a long-distance truck driver, was eastbound on Interstate 70. A woman driving westbound had suddenly lapsed into a diabetic coma. Her car crossed over the median and two lanes of traffic, and then hit his truck. Avery sustained two broken legs, a broken arm, and multiple internal injuries.

Avery had wanted to leave his job for something that would allow him to have more free time at home. But he never allowed himself to do this because he believed that his father and grandfather, both career truck drivers, would think less of him. After the accident, he resigned himself to getting back on the road as soon as possible—not because he wanted to, but because his father and grandfather "would have done the same thing." A year later, Avery was killed in a crash on Interstate 70.

David, United States

"I asked myself, 'What is the worst that can happen to me by starting my own business?' I took the leap and my business took off!"

David had worked as a mechanical engineer since graduating from college. While flying to a nearby city on business, David's airplane was forced to make an unscheduled landing due to mechanical difficulties. He noticed a young mother struggling to gather up her two babies, stroller, and diaper bag as they were exiting the plane. An idea suddenly flashed into his brain.

David and a coworker developed the idea to manufacture a travel product for parents called the Cosie Carry-On, a one-piece luggage system that combined a carry-on bag, diaper bag, and stroller. The project took only five months from initial concept to patent approval. The success of this project gave

> Vision without action is a daydream.
> Action without vision is a nightmare.
>
> Japanese proverb

Dave the courage he needed to leave the company that he had relied on for so many years for financial security. He and his partner formed their own company through which to develop other products.

WERNER, GERMANY

Werner, a commercial airline pilot, successfully overcame his mother's message that marriage was "a dead end street." At the age of 40, Werner married for the first time.

PATRICIA, UNITED STATES

Patricia was a successful real estate agent and single mother to her sixteen-year-old son, Anthony. She was working hard to earn enough money for his upcoming college education. At 12:40 A.M. on December 31, 1996, Anthony was killed when the car that he and four other high school friends were riding in hit a truck at an intersection in Tampa, Florida.

When Patricia received the news that her son had died, life, as she thought she knew it, ended.

"The very thought of living my life without Anthony was unfathomable. Since the pain of a future without him was too much to bear, I was forced into staying in the present moment. This was an entirely new place for me, since I had always lived my life in 'future tense.'"

Anthony's death prompted Patricia to review her life. She realized "all things external" had been driving her life and that she had been held captive by that point of view.

"I suddenly knew that if I didn't heal my heart, if I didn't go inside to find out who I was, I would get stuck like so many people who had lost a loved one," she recalls. "For me, that would have been like dying a long, slow death."

"Anthony's sudden passing just as suddenly shifted the way I perceived life, myself, and my relationships. It flung open a door to a conscious life lived in the present moment. It taught me that the present moment is the place where life, in truth, really exists."

Patricia eventually left the real estate business to open The Inspired Heart, a metaphysical bookstore and healing center.

MOTHER TERESA, INDIA

"By the end of 1952, the third floor of the Gomeses' family house had become too small for the community of twenty-six members. Mother Teresa was obliged to look for a larger home to accommodate the increasing number of sisters. After storming heaven with prayer, she found a house on Lower Circular Road that is still today the motherhouse of the Missionaries of Charity. The community moved there in February 1953.

The inspiration of 1946 was now a "living reality"—a flourishing community serving the poorest of the poor of Calcutta." (From *Mother Teresa, Come Be My Light*; *The private writings of the "Saint of Calcutta,"* edited and with commentary by Brian Kolodiejchuk, M.C.)

REBECCA, UNITED STATES

Rebecca was attending a University to acquire her Bachelor of Science degree in Nursing. During her annual medical checkup, doctors discovered a lump on her thyroid gland that required surgery for removal. On the day that she was to be released after surgery, Rebecca called

Rick, her husband, but couldn't get an answer. She dozed in and out of sleep that day, waiting for him to arrive. Each time she awoke, she asked the nurses if he had arrived to pick her up. The last time she awoke to inquire again, the doctor and nurses came into her room and gave her news that split her apart: Rick had shot himself in the parking lot of the hospital.

Rebecca remembers: "He left a note asking my forgiveness and telling me that he couldn't live without me. Rick was a warm, caring people-pleaser. He had experienced depression in short bouts throughout our married life. For some reason, he thought I was going to leave him when I became a nurse. For all that he said in the note, I was left without the chance to reply."

"I got into another relationship much too quickly. I grabbed it in order to have stability at a very unstable time of my life. If I had it to do over again, I would have remained single for a longer time to give my son the undivided attention he needed. I think what I am really saying is that I needed to give myself some undivided attention."

ANGELA, UNITED STATES

Angela and her new husband, John, ran a thriving antiques import business. She had two daughters from a previous marriage and both girls lived with her and John. Suddenly, the oldest daughter, Christiana, decided that she wanted to live with Angela's ex-husband. This separation was painful for Angela and she experienced overwhelming anxiety and sadness.

While on a business trip to Thailand with John, Angela became pregnant. At thirty-nine, with two teenage daughters and now experiencing separation from Christiana, Angela knew that she was emotionally incapable of having another child at this time in her life.

"The business that John and I were running was thriving and, besides my girls, my work was my passion," Angela says. "When I became pregnant, I felt cornered and tied up. I was a mother, an ex-wife, a wife, and a business owner. Something told me that to become a mother again would destroy a greater creative potential which was now flowering in me. Ultimately, I had an abortion. As I look back on that time I see that life was challenging me to decide where I most wanted to direct my energies."

BONNIE, UNITED STATES

Bonnie worked as a finance manager at an auto dealership. It was a difficult time in her life because she was raising two sons without financial support from her ex-husband, and she was demoralized by the drug problems and truancy episodes of one of her sons.

"Every time I turned around there would be another upset that caused chaos," she says. "I was providing the entire emotional support for all of my family members so work became my place to become a different person, a place where I could excel and be acknowledged."

With her manager's support, Bonnie found self-esteem and viability. Slowly but surely, she embraced a new future. She left the auto dealership to work at a local television station where she did something she had always dreamed of doing—hosting her own television show.

McKenzie's Journal

January 3, 1992 • Corporate demands these last six months have been intense. Bill has completed facilitating the Initial Public Offering of the company's stock on the Japanese Stock Exchange—an extraordinary, but stressful, feat.

We have seldom argued before, but now we are at it almost every day. I hate it because I love him so much and I know that he loves me. He is demanding the return of the spouse who signed up to support him here. The truth is, he wants me for himself but there's another me being pulled beyond my personal will into the unknown.

January 12, 1992 • Bill comes home from work early this afternoon. Something's bothering him, but I can't get it out of him. His silence has become frequent. I can only think that it must be about me.

January 20, 1992 • What has been bothering Bill finally comes out today: he wants to go home. He tells me that he's accomplished everything he came to Japan to do. He says it's time to end the assignment and repatriate to the States.

February 12, 1992 • Bill won't give me any details of what is actually transpiring for his new position back at corporate headquarters. From my place on the sidelines, it has been a long, drawn-out negotiation. He's been working his calculator constantly. It's obvious that it's not just the challenge of the job—it's the money. It seems way too important to him, especially since, at least to me anyway, we have more than enough.

February 18, 1992 • Bill tells me that he will return to headquarters as a Senior Vice President in the International Division. He seems happy to have another challenge, but every morning he deplores getting dressed for work. It's always been that way with him. Is he happy? Is he not happy? Are any corporate robots truly happy?

March 6, 1992 • We arrive back in Michigan knowing that we will never return to Japan. It's bittersweet because I realize what Japan has done for me and how it has changed me. The thought of being at the cabin and with Ciao gives us the energy to drive the two hours north despite our fatigue from the twenty-two hour trip. When we drive through the gate at the Club, we find the road as deeply rutted with ice and snow as it was the first time we saw the cabin together seven years ago. At the caretaker's house Ciao bounds out to meet us…I am so happy to see her! I will never again have to say ciao to Ciao!

In the cold, white silence of late winter is the same silence I found in the shrines and temples. If I have learned one thing about silence, it's that it is where all the answers are found. What I still lack is the discipline to let my mind surrender to it on a consistent basis.

> It is not necessary to change. Survival is not mandatory.
> W. Edwards Deming

March 10, 1992 • Anniversary day…our first date was breakfast at the Cascade Inn. With all the world travel and experiences that I have had since then, I feel like I've lived an entire lifetime in just seven years.

March 11, 1992 • Bill is eager to get back to business affairs at headquarters. I'm not surprised. We drive down to Grand Rapids to the house.

March 12, 1992 • Sleeping in the house last night gave me an unsettled feeling. Everything here seems to have been in a state of suspended animation since we departed for Japan. I walk Bill out to the car as he leaves for work. He turns the key in the ignition and kisses me at the same time. Some people love the what in their life more than the whom. Is this necessarily a bad thing? Can I be satisfied as the mistress to the work he considers his wife?

The house is stagnant from sitting unoccupied for three-and-a-half years. Our personal belongings will not arrive from overseas for at least a month. I open a dresser drawer to look for something to wear. The clothes I had left behind are still neatly folded in short and perfect "McKenzie stacks." I pull out a shirt and hold it up in front of me in the mirror. I don't recognize myself. Who was I then? More to the point, who am I now?

March 16, 1992 • Seven years ago today Bill drove me "up north" to see the cabin for the first time. He had waited nine years for it to come up for sale, and within just two weeks of our first meeting, it did.

March 20, 1992 • We return to our usual weekend commute between the house and the cabin. I snowshoe with Ciao to visit all of our favorite places in the woods. One particular place has a strong pull on me. Twin Creek winds back and forth through the property as it flows out of the larger of our two lakes. On its way, it runs under an ancient white pine that, when it was young, might have been blown over in a windstorm. It now leans from its original home on one bank with its thick roots arching high above ground across the stream into the embrace of some cedars on the other side that "caught it." Its thick roots are loosely woven in a woody web and form a bridge over the creek. I lie across it and gaze through the spaces into the flowing water beneath. On the opposite shore, three white cedar trees support the old pine, creating a timber tent.

Ciao and I come here first today. I crawl on my hands and knees out over the root bridge and step onto the opposite creek bank. There's a large mound covered with snow in the "tent." I squat beside it and brush away the snow to see what it is: a lone fawn is curled in a peaceful repose, its nose tucked into its soft belly fur. Suddenly the winter sounds of the woods fall away to a silence that I have never experienced. It is the deep, eternal silence of death.

March 29, 1992 • Today I read a flyer at the bookstore about a lecture tomorrow at a Jung Society meeting at Fountain Street Church. A woman from Santa Fe, New Mexico, is scheduled to speak about "the Higher Self." I recall the sessions that I'd had. I find the transcripts tucked away in a box in the loft. It's been almost two years but the images and lessons in each transcript are as fresh as when I was there in the session experience. As I read them again, I notice things that had escaped me until now. I am on fire.

March 30, 1992 • I sit in the front row of the lecture room at Fountain Street Church. As it turns out, Ana is a facilitator of the same type of inner journeywork that I did at the Light Institute in Santa Fe. She took her training at the Deva Foundation, not far from there in Glorieta, also dedicated to the work of psycho-spiritual development. After the lecture, I arrange to work with her here in Michigan.

April 3, 1992 • Ciao is five years old today. We sit on the floor and I surround her with bones of all shapes and sizes, seeing which one she chooses first. Like a good Lab, she grabs all that she can hold in her mouth at once. Good doggie.

Bill buys a three-year-old German Shorthair pointer for bird hunting. Her name is Dana and she is a most beautiful and loving dog. She and Ciao fall in love with each other and play constantly. I can see how grateful Dana is to have a real home, since she's been living in a training kennel for her entire life. I have no words for what I feel when I watch her explore her new world. The ice is off the lakes at the cabin. The loons will return soon and we will hear them call day and night. I live for their calls.

April 15, 1992 • Bill's 51st birthday. We celebrate with all of our in-town friends, most of who also work for the corporation. The after-dinner conversation comes around, as it always does, to work. Not everybody is as happy in the corporation as they once were when it was smaller in size.

April 21, 1992 • Bill is having a moral dilemma with the corporate environment under the new management. It has gone the way of brash business school guys with big guns terminating employees through e-mail. The politics are rough and the employees are adrift in confusion and mistrust. I find Bill in the living room in the middle of the night trying to come to terms with it all. His take is that the company has lost its heart by virtue of its heft.

April 29, 1992 • Bill is no longer able to stomach the environment at work. I think that this has everything to do with the stomach problems he was just in the hospital for recently. All he's doing is putting out fires set by the owners' kids who now occupy the top management positions. The problem is that as a Senior V.P., he has to spend his days in this snake pit.

May 12, 1992 • At the cabin. During our lunch on the deck Bill tells me that he might want to take early retirement. I'm ecstatic about the idea, but he seems to be less sure. I say yes; he says maybe. He brings out the calculator. His angst about having enough money is ridiculous. If he only realized how much he's got, money not included....

May 13, 1992 • Bill and I have more discussion about his work. There are zero reasons I can think of for him to stay at the company if he no longer enjoys it. Twenty-five years is enough. I try to tell him that there are limitless other things he can do. I would love for him to be free of the stress.

May 14, 1992 • I kayak over the big lake with Ciao swimming off the bow. The loons are on the nest!

May 19, 1992 • Bill has decided to quit the company. I am thrilled!

May 22-25, 1992 • I travel downstate to do Higher Self work with Ana. It's a three-hour drive each way, but I don't complain since many people travel halfway around the world to do this work here in the States. I love going inside myself to experience all that is there. The most important thing this work accomplishes is to connect me to a reservoir of "knowing." Everything that I need to know is there. From it, I can access answers that heretofore have escaped me. Moreover, I'm coming away from each session with an incredible inner stability.

I am also touching long hidden wounds, fear, narrow-mindedness, and self-judgment. Although there is "housecleaning" to be done, I am more and more eager to free myself of the patterns that obscure what my life is really supposed to mean and be. The Higher Self replaces the muddle of my conflicts and confusions with higher order.

This healing work goes far beyond the conventional therapy that I've had in the past: it gives me access to higher-source guidance and insight and simultaneously releases the self-limiting status quo patterns that have held me hostage. My Higher Self knows precisely how to help me overcome fear, negative emotions, and judgment. Higher perspective replaces limited perspective and dissolves self-limiting themes within patterns. My body is lighter and my mind calmer after each session. The neck pain that I've had for years is suddenly gone because the themes that have been stuck there are now being released.

> The only difference between a rut and a grave are their dimensions.
>
> Ellen Glascow

June 1, 1992 • The loons lose their one, precious egg to the eagle.

June 2, 1992 • Bill will serve as an outside consultant to the company for one year. I can't tell if he's happy or not.

June 13, 1992 • As I continue to dive into myself with inner work, Bill makes himself busy with projects at home and cabin. Dana's puppies are due any day.

June 15, 1992 • Dana begins birthing her puppies shortly after 3 A.M. There are a total of six, with one stillbirth. Ciao is very interested in all of this but keeps a polite distance from the whelping box.

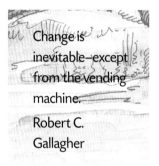

Change is inevitable—except from the vending machine.

Robert C. Gallagher

July 3, 1992 • The loons hatch two chicks from their second mating. Wow!

July 4, 1992 • The puppies are fantastic— it's total fun taking care of them. The runt is the only female in the litter. I name her Kiwi for the next country that Bill and I want to visit—New Zealand!

July 28, 1992 • Three times each day I float in my kayak and watch the loon parents with their chicks. They have relocated them from the big lake to the little lake and now we can watch them from the dock. One chick is a bit smaller and I can see how it has to make considerably more effort to do the things that its sibling does easily.

August 3, 1992 • Bill has run out of household projects and boredom has set in. With so many possibilities, I fail to see how he can be bored. And despite so many other companies wanting him to work for them, he has resisted, not wanting to "start all over again," as he puts it. He seems stuck.

August 6, 1992 • Ana suggests that in September I go to the Deva Foundation in Santa Fe for a workshop. I want to become a facilitator of the work that I have been doing with her and can apply for the training program when I am there. How to tell Bill and have it feel good to him? What a struggle it is to stand alone with what I want to do while being married to a guy who thinks my being his wife is enough. I love him but can't get it through to him that being free to do what I love will actually add to our relationship, not subtract from it. I cannot live any longer on what I am. I can only live for what I must become.

August 9, 1992 • Bill is unenthusiastic, to say the least, about my attending the workshop. What do I do? Appease him and not go … and then die for the rest of my life?

Since leaving the company he needs me to be around all the time. It feels burdensome. He's not as strong and independent as he seemed to be while he was working. Was his work holding him up like I now have to?

September 12, 1992 • I am at the Deva Foundation in Glorieta, near Santa Fe, with people from other countries who are participating in the workshop. Our diverse cultural backgrounds serve to make us interesting to each other. I will spend a week here and hopefully qualify for the facilitator-training program that begins next spring.

September 17, 1992 • I am accepted into the facilitator-training program that begins next March! When I think about actually making the commitment, I get nervous. I want to step onto this path, but I'm also eager to get home to Bill. Comfort with the known is suddenly struggling with fear of the unknown. I am torn down the absolute middle.

Your vision will become clear only when you look into your heart.

Carl Jung

September 18, 1992 • Bill hunts upland birds with his buddies. I kayak to watch the loons. They have grown from tiny, down-covered chicks into adolescents able to swim and find food on their own.

September 20, 1992 • The male loon has left for its East Coast wintering grounds, leaving the female and twin chicks behind. She is teaching them how to fly—the lessons are amazing to observe.

October 11, 1992 • The female loon has migrated, leaving the young ones behind to complete their flight practice. I have been watching them over the last few weeks as they perform take-offs and landings, flapping their wings wildly as they peddle across the surface of the water to get airborne. The effort it takes seems enormous. This will be their first and last year at Twin Lakes. Reaching the East Coast in late October, they will spend the next four years growing to maturity. Then will they return north to join the annual cycle of mating and migrating with the seasons.

I recall how, five years ago, a yearling loon was not able to migrate and was forced to winter over on Lake Michigan. The next spring it returned to Twin Lakes and when the adults returned to mate, they killed it by driving it onto the shore. A loon out of water does not survive.

October 15, 1992 • The smaller loon is not doing as well in flight practice. It can get airborne, but can only fly for a short distance before it drops down onto the water. What's wrong with it? How will it be able to migrate if it cannot fly out on its own?

November 2, 1992 • The bigger twin has left for its wintering grounds. The smaller loon is still unable to fly. My heart aches for its weakness and vulnerability. I am afraid for it.

November 4, 1992 • The days are short and cold now. I can still paddle over to the big lake every day to see if my little loon has been able to depart. But it remains, still floundering but still trying.

November 6, 1992 • Dense, dark clouds hover low as winter begins in earnest. Here, so close to the Lake Michigan shoreline, we will rarely see the sun until late March. I watch helplessly as a thin layer of ice begins to form around the edges of the lake. What is going to become of the little loon?

November 9, 1992 • For the first time in his life, Bill has no interest in deer hunting. We decide to spend the winter skiing in Colorado. I snowshoe over to the big lake one last time to see if the little loon has made it out. Freezing temperatures these last three nights have iced over the entire surface of the lake except for a small opening at the northwest corner. It is here that I find the loon paddling in tight circles from edge to edge. If it is forced onto shore, it will die. I break ice from the shore out to the middle of the lake with the kayak so that it can dive into deep water for food.

November 10, 1992 • We pack our gear and the dogs into the car and head west to Durango. My tortured heart keeps looking back toward the little loon left by itself to survive against formidable odds. I know its fate belongs to nature, but I still want to intervene, to hold off the death that I know is certain.

November 15, 1992 • Bill is restless. He's already unexcited about skiing and uncomfortable about living in an unfamiliar house. I am uncomfortable with him being uncomfortable.

November 16, 1992 • All Bill wants to do is to go back to work at the company. Unfortunately, that is no longer an option. All he talks about is having made "the mistake of his life" by retiring. There is nothing that I can say to make him feel better. My helplessness is unbearable.

November 19, 1992 • Dejection, sadness, and inertia in Bill. He does not receive well my suggestion that he get some kind of medication. He assures me that it's temporary and that he can "handle it." He is so hooked on going back to a company (a life?) that he can't go back to. He won't say why he doesn't want to work for any of the other companies that have been pursuing him. He says less and less every day. I don't know what to do.

November 22, 1992 • I suggest Bill go to Johns Hopkins Hospital. Nothing doing. Instead, and amazingly, he wants to go to Santa Fe for Higher Self work at the Deva Foundation. He feels that if the sessions give me so much peace and direction it can do the same for him.

November 24, 1992 • Bill and I meet with Ana at Deva Foundation. Over the next four days she will facilitate him and me in separate sessions. Before my first session, Ana and I also talk about my acceptance into the facilitator-training program.

November 26, 1992 • The Alameda Inn is a wonderful place to stay while we are here. I am hoping that Bill will love Santa Fe enough to come here with me in March while I am in training.

My Higher Self sessions are every morning, and Bill's are in the afternoons. We do not talk about the specific details of our sessions but we do talk about the themes and patterns that our Higher Selves have brought to our awareness for healing.

November 30, 1992 • We drive back to Durango. From his sessions Bill has come to an understanding of his mother's influence over his life. He shares with me that he's always hated her constant demands of his time, attention, and money; he has always tolerated it as being his duty to her. His father was a tractor mechanic and that had been a disappointment to his mom. Instead, she molded Bill into her ideal image, her success story. Her expectation for Bill was to light up her small-town persona with his corporate accomplishments and to bestow her with status by association. Regardless of how far from home he traveled, her psychic hold on him was always there. Now he knows that she steered his life into her unfulfilled dreams for herself.

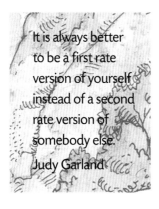

It is always better to be a first rate version of yourself instead of a second rate version of somebody else.

Judy Garland

December 1, 1992 • It comes as no surprise to either one of us to hear his mother's voice on the phone recorder the day of our return to Durango from Santa Fe. She has called to tell him that she is dying and needs him to come home right away. Ana told him that this was likely to happen.

December 5, 1992 • Miles of interstate concrete disappear beneath the van as we drive home. Bill frets about what to do for his mother. The dogs take turns licking our hands.

December 6, 1992 • We arrive at the cabin exhausted. I am already waking up exhausted every morning as it is and I don't know why.

December 7, 1992 • Bill calls his mother this morning and finds out that she is not dying at all; her plea has turned out to be just another ploy for his attention. He pulls back, angrier than I have ever seen him. Now he can really see the sticky web of emotional incest.

I learn from the caretaker, Jim, that an ermine caught the little loon at the open springs near the northwest corner of the lake. Anguish.

December 27, 1992 • We spend my fortieth birthday and Christmas with the dogs at the cabin. For one of the few times in his life, Bill decides that we will not go to his family's for Christmas. They aren't happy and I stay out of it.

January 1, 1993 • Bill and I drive down to the house after spending New Year's Eve with friends at the cabin.

January 27, 1993 • Bill sees a psychiatrist and brings home antidepressant medication. I feel relieved. He feels diminished.

January 28, 1993 • This morning Bill wakes up so shaky he can't even dial the phone. It takes a while for us to figure out that it may be due to the medication he started last night. I call the doctor immediately. What is happening?

January 29, 1993 • The psychiatrist cuts the dosage in half. I still want Bill to go to Johns Hopkins University Hospital instead of this guy. Bill refuses to go; he just wants to go to the cabin collect himself.

February 7, 1993 • Bill writes every morning. He asks me to facilitate him in Higher Self sessions to bring into awareness what may be still stuck inside him. I transcribe every word as he narrates what he experiences within. Surprisingly, there emerges unresolved grief in losing Lucci when he was forty years old. He was going to marry her, but she died in a car accident on the way home from his cabin one morning. Then, forgotten childhood dreams surface, precious dreams paved several times over with parental prerogatives. He cries tears of grief in having lost those dreams, and cries tears of joy in finally reclaiming them.

February 10, 1993 • Lack of direction. Inertia. These are the worst. I encourage Bill to get together with friends in Grand Rapids because he's too isolated here at the cabin. He has another appointment with the shrink, even though he stopped taking the meds.

February 13, 1993 • I decide to cancel my facilitator training but Bill refuses to allow me to back out of it. What do I do? I cannot leave him right now. He is the love of my life.

February 15, 1993 • Last night Bill dreams about seeing his friend, John Denver, performing at a concert. In the dream, John gives Bill a ticket to his performance. Performance. How devastating it must be to realize that you are performing your life instead of living it.

February 18, 1993 • Last night Bill dreams that his sister is killed in a car crash. This really frightens him.

February 20, 1993 • Bill feels better today. He has lunch today with old friends from the company and I have lunch with Diane.

February 21, 1993 • Bill is back on the tennis court. I'm getting myself ready for Santa Fe.

February 23, 1993 • We have lunch at the Thornapple Village Inn. Bill has put together some ideas of what he wants us to do when I complete my training. It's great to have that in front of us, but I still wish he'd come with me to Santa Fe. I ask him to surprise me and fly down in April to celebrate his birthday—number 52!

February 27, 1993 • I leave for Santa Fe tomorrow. We sit in front of the fire this evening; Bill reads while I write. Through the window we become aware of deer moving slowly towards the cabin. Some emerge from the woods, others come up from the lake, and others come down the path in twos and threes. Speechless, we count nineteen in all and watch them wander around the cabin. It's magic that this is happening on my last night here.

February 28, 1993 • On the way to the airport with Ciao, we drop Dana off for training at the hunting preserve. I think Bill should keep her for companionship while I'm gone, but according to him this is the only time of the year that the trainer can give her undivided attention.

At the airport, Ciao fixes her eyes on us as her crate rattles away on the conveyor downstairs to cargo. I hate that I have to fly her but Art assures me that Northwest does the best job in transporting animals. It's nice to have a pilot for a brother.

While the other passengers board, Bill holds me and promises to call every day. I'm bothered by the fact that he won't agree come to Santa Fe. All I can think is that he's got to be uncomfortable with what I'm doing. I'm hyperventilating with anxiety.

He kisses me and tells me that I'm going to be a great doctor someday and that he's proud of me. His last kiss is short and strange, but there's no time to ask why. The jetway door closes as I look back at him.

Sherpa Norbu's Parable

I walk silently alongside Shaypa as she treks steadily upward. Her steps are taking her toward the summit.

Taking time to stop and rest, she drops her backpack on the rocky ground and sits beside it, relieved to finally have it off. Looking back in the direction from which she has come, she notices that the path has disappeared behind her! Shaypa realizes that forward, toward the summit, is the only direction she can continue.

Her weariness suddenly seems out of proportion for where she is on her journey. There is something wrong with her pack: it's too heavy. Shaypa reaches into it, sifting through its contents for the first time since she began her trek. She unexpectedly sees things in that don't belong to her!

"Why am I carrying others' stuff up this mountain?" she moans. She realizes that if she is to make it to the summit she'll have to remove some things from her backpack.

"But how can I determine what really belongs to me and what does not?" She doesn't know where to begin because the task seems so overwhelming.

She begins in the simplest way possible, by carefully removing everything from the pack and placing each piece on the ground around her.

"Do you see these small objects?" I ask, pointing to the objects lying next to her. "Do you see how they cast a light outward from within themselves?"

"Does that mean they belong to me?"

"Yes," I reply. "The things that are truly yours will attract your attention to the light from their interior. They are the only things that you will need for your journey."

Shaypa regards the few, but precious items. "Notice how they shine like tiny lanterns as they sit all around you," I say.

When Shaypa looks for the pieces of others' lives that she has unpacked, she finds that they have vanished without a trace. "It is vital that you leave them behind," I advise her. "Otherwise, you will not have the energy to reach your summit."

Despite the fact that night has fallen, Shaypa decides that she can continue up the mountain in the dark because she has the precious pieces of herself illuminating her path. She can move ahead with ease with her true self to light her way.

As she climbs higher, Shaypa realizes that it doesn't matter how many or how few pieces she has in her backpack. The most important thing is that she now carries what is truly hers. Her pack is light because her essence is Light. And being so is a welcome relief.

Shaypa remembers her true nature as a child. She begins to walk as she did as a child: trusting her steps, trusting her direction, even trusting the unknown. She senses that life has been guiding her precisely to this place, at this time, to discover these precious pieces of herself.

Guided by her inner lanterns, Shaypa walks with sure steps until sunrise. As she approaches the next cairn, an eagle appears carrying the sound of the wind—a low hum—in its wings. This sound, unlike any other, is the voice of Spirit, and Shaypa suddenly realizes that it is calling to her! The eagle seizes Shaypa by the crown of her head, pulling her skyward. She sees the world she once knew transformed into another. Once it is certain that her vision is as clear as its own, the eagle releases her, inviting her to fly with it. She flails and flaps awkwardly at first, unable to figure how to stay airborne without a lot of effort.

"Have you asked me to fly before I am really ready?" she wails. The eagle urges her to go higher. She discovers that her flight becomes calmer the higher she goes. Shaypa accepts her role as apprentice in her first flight under the eagle's protective wings. Here in these wings Shaypa hears her true voice in the sacred song of Spirit.

They ascend even higher to arrive at a place of a most profound silence. It is the place where Shaypa's higher life purpose was born. The eagle pulls her to itself. As they merge, the power of the message and the power of the messenger become one. Shaypa has met the love of her life.

She realizes that the eagle has been inside of her all along, waiting for the precise time to invite her to be its messenger. The sound in its wings can now sing its vision through her voice—an authentic voice that the world will surely hear and love because Shaypa is in love. And who does not love one who is in love?

ON WINGS OF THOUGHT

On wings of thought
we fly,
sweeping with the eagle's upward
climb
to mountain heights in cool
thin airs,
or fluttering as sparrows
in the dust,
scattering twigs of old
to left and right.
And yet
so versatile the form,
so rich the creativity,
our deepest knowing
can give birth to worlds.

How swift the message
passes
that leaps the tender endings
of our nerves,
and trips the signal's
instantaneous flash.
And so a vision released
goes winging
as a dove before the hawk,
swooping outward from
the opened cage
of mind,
bursting from our skulls
to freedom,
that cannot be confined,
once it has flown.

CHERRY EARLE, NEW ZEALAND

CRISIS OF POWER

The Motive is in the Mirror

THE TERRITORY

The ability, skill, or capacity to do something

YOUR APPROXIMATE AGE

North Travel Group	(1936-1946)	46-41
South Travel Group	(1947-1957)	41-37
East Travel Group	(1958-1968)	37-36
West Travel Group	(1969-1979)	36-37

TIME IN TRANSIT

Up to two years

WHAT TO PACK OR ACQUIRE ALONG THE WAY

Physical:	Regeneration
Mental:	Impeccability
Emotional:	Honesty
Spiritual:	Forgiveness

WHAT TO LEAVE BEHIND

The win-lose paradigm

THE WEATHER FORECAST

Seismic activity

THE MANTRA

Mirror, mirror on the wall, do I use my power for the benefit of all?

TRAVEL ITINERARY

Power is life force energy. Action is life force energy, or power, in motion. Every action forms the basis of your interactions and affects both yourself and others, known or unknown to you.

Actions arise from motives, both conscious and unconscious, and create your future circumstances. Balanced motives create balanced actions, resulting in balanced future circumstances. Unbalanced motives create unbalanced actions, resulting in unbalanced future circumstances.

Since the source of life force energy is universally available to everyone, the power it bestows is to be universally used by and for all. To use power in a balanced way is to act for the benefit of both yourself and others—you benefit when, by your actions, others benefit. To use power in an unbalanced way is to seek power for selfish means or to abandon your power. Using your power in an unbalanced way dissipates your life force energy. Either way, when the effect of your past or present actions comes home to roost at some point in the future, you may discover that your free will choice to act in either a balanced or unbalanced way can be your future best friend or your future fiercest foe.

The Crisis of Power can present you with some trying topography. You may experience endings, loss, disruptions, breakdowns, and upheavals. These events may be challenging, messy, or even nightmarish—life is asking you to clear away the inner debris that these outer events are mirroring. You may find that you have little or no control over events that take place now.

The heart of the person before you is a mirror. See there your own form.

Ko-ji-ki Hachiman Kasuga

You can be either aware or unaware that you may need to change some things about yourself. You can be either resistant to change or motivated to change. During this crisis, others may enable your resistance to change, or attempt to prevent you from making needed changes. Still others will support you as you make needed changes. Choose your friends and associates wisely!

In addition to being universal, the forces behind the Crisis of Power are also absolute. That is, any resistance to necessary change guarantees suffering. But, when you agree to change, you activate the exact resources from within yourself that create positive flow in your life. The best way to trek this terrain is with transparency, impeccability, and forgiveness of yourself and others. These are balanced attributes, so by applying them, you are creating positive future circumstances for yourself!

The Crisis of Power also acts to unearth your deepest needs and desires, but they might be so deeply buried that you are unaware of them. Any "earthquakes" that occur during the Crisis of Power are for the purpose of bringing these needs and desires to the surface so that you and your higher life purpose can thrive.

ESSENTIAL TRAVEL TIPS

- Look squarely at crisis events and take responsibility for your part by identifying and transforming your underlying motives.

- Accept what cannot be changed. Let go of whatever is out of your control.

- Heal disturbing emotions. This helps you to regain your life force energy, or power.

- Step out of relationships with anything or anyone whose motives are counter to the universal mandate of "for the benefit of others."

- Forgive yourself and others. The act of forgiveness returns power to the victim, restoring their life force energy.

- Choose to use your power to benefit others. This requires maintaining conscious awareness of your motives.

- To know true power you must first become aware that you have access to it. True power comes from only one place—the Source. Accessing true power from the Source gives you a natural and spontaneous inclination to use it for the greater good. It is within.

- Trust your Higher Self to help you find and walk the high road through this tremendous, but sometimes treacherous, terrain.

The Ultimate Travel Tip:

True power is not invisible—it is transparent. And it is found only within.

Do not believe in anything simply because you have heard it.
Do not believe in anything simply because it is
spoken and rumored by many.
Do not believe in anything simply because it is
found written in your religious books.
Do not believe in anything merely on the
authority of your teachers and elders.
Do not believe in traditions because they have been
handed down for many generations.
But after observation and analysis, when you find that
anything agrees with reason and is conducive to the good and
benefit of one and all, then accept it and live up to it.

Buddha

SIGHTS AND SOUNDS

This is a short list of just some of the things that you may encounter along the way through the Crisis of Power. You can recognize them as personal traits or as symbolic messages in your dreams. You are free to choose which can be of real and lasting assistance for your journey.

Atrocities	Dishonesty	Jealousy	Release
Betrayal	Envy	Manipulation	Resurrection
Callousness	Evasion	Masochism	Sadism
Catastrophes	Fanaticism	Morality	Secrecy
Chasms	Fatality	Mortality	Sexuality
Concealment	Forgiveness	Mysticism	Spiritual inquiry
Conspiracy	Grief	Obsession	Transformation
Contempt	Guilt	Passion	Transparency
Control	Hidden forces	Purification	Turning points
Corruption	Honesty	Quagmires	Underhandedness
Crime	Immorality	Rape	Violence
Death	Indifference	Rebirth	Victims
Debauchery	Insurances	Regeneration	Victimizers
Defilement	Lawlessness	Reincarnation	Vindictiveness
Destitution	Liars	Resentment	
Destruction	Healing	Rejuvenation	

Think hard about the motive behind each and every choice you make, and hope that the effect of those choices is one that you'll be able to live with later on.

Beverly Peshaba Hill, great granddaughter of Chief Ben Peshaba, Eagle Clan of the Odawa Nation

Traveling Companions

Mother Teresa, India

Mother Teresa received the Pope John XXIII Peace Prize. She accepted this on behalf of the poor, using the money to fund her centers.

Princess Diana, England

Diana, Princess of Wales, died after a car crash in Paris, France, on August 31, 1997.

Mary, Canada

Mary had been married to a wealthy businessman since her early twenties. With the wealth acquired from his career, they led a life of luxury, easily satisfying their every material desire. Then Mary was diagnosed with post-polio syndrome, and while she was undergoing physical therapy, she became interested in becoming a physiotherapist. Her new interest diverted attention from her husband. He tried to dissuade her from attending college to obtain her degree. Knowing that she was financially dependent on him, he threatened to divorce her if she chose school over him. Instead, Mary divorced him and paid for her tuition with student loans and two part-time jobs.

Xin, China

Xin was passionate about her work as a fashion designer, but was married to a man who was threatened by her growing professional success. The more creative she became in her work, the more he would attempt to diminish her sense of self-esteem at home. "I saw the darker side of my husband's fear," Xin said, and "was shocked at how he chose to undermine me. Ultimately, our relationship self-destructed under the weight of our power battles."

Alberto, Mexico

Alberto worked in marketing at a large corporation. "One of my co-workers constantly bent company rules to her personal benefit and career furtherance," he recalls. "It was also frustrating to be used as a pawn in her power games. I eventually requested a transfer to another department — a scary thing for me to do because I was under financial pressure to support my children. But to my total surprise (and relief) my new job turned out to be a much better position!"

KARYN, DENMARK

Karyn married an electronics engineer after the death of her husband in hopes that he would bring financial and emotional stability to her life. He was not a warm, fatherly type and they had definite and different ideas about how to raise her son and her desire to continue her education. Because he earned a higher salary, she allowed him to dictate the decisions about these issues.

"At a certain point I realized that I could not stop being the mother of my son and I could not stop being an intelligent woman capable of attaining an advanced degree. I had to do a difficult but necessary thing: contribute an equal financial contribution to our marriage, even though it required me to work longer hours. This allowed me to avoid being dominated and controlled through the power of his income. The freedom I originally sought by marrying him turned out to be a subtle form of self-captivity. I was actually subverting my own power! I came to realize that I, myself, could provide the financial and emotional stability I had married my husband for."

McKenzie's Journal

February 25, 1993 • I find my seat and anxiously wait for the flight attendant to bring the certificate that confirms that Ciao is safely onboard. I'm sick with worry about her in the cargo hold.

I look for Bill in the concourse window as the plane leaves the gate. He's gone. I feel a sharp stab in my solar plexus—I'm afraid of being alone in my own shoes.

The plane circles over the New Mexico desert to make its landing in Albuquerque. More pangs of worry. Am I doing the right thing by coming down here?

In baggage claim, I wait for what seems to be too long for Ciao to be brought up from cargo. Where is my dog? What dogs do for us humans is unbelievably humbling. A man pushing her crate finally appears, and she bounds out shouting for me and at me. I understand. I present food as a peace offering.

Arriving at the casita I call Bill before unpacking my suitcases. There's no answer. I'll call him later. Ciao is already outside exploring. That's another thing about dogs — resiliency. I take a lesson. Bill calls me and we talk for half an hour.

February 26, 1993 • Now I'm here and less sure of myself than I thought I'd be. But there's only one direction. I have to go forward with this training. Life will not happen any other way.

February 27, 1993 • I drive around Santa Fe with Ciao, locating the hiking trails. After lunch we hike in the mountains behind St. John's College. I'm going to make sure that she has as good a time here as me.

February 28, 1993 • This evening I make a fire with pinion wood and talk with Bill on the phone. He played tennis with some friends today and will head back up to the cabin tomorrow. We agree to talk on the phone every other day. It helps.

March 1, 1993 • First day of facilitator training at the Deva Foundation! Ciao and I arrive forty-five minutes early so that I can take her for a long walk in the meadow before morning class. I'm relieved to be able to bring her to class every day. Rick and Rachel, the teachers, make room for all beings. I'm fortunate to have found these people. I keep the Jeep's back hatch open for her to come and go on the grounds around the classroom building. It's like her personal camper. Cool!

There are eleven of us in the training—from Denmark, Belgium, Germany, Switzerland, and the United States. I don't even know my classmates yet, but I feel a deep connection to them–not just by virtue of the experiences we will share over the next two months, but because they are my world sisters and brothers.

March 6, 1993 • The first week of my training has gone by quickly. I call Bill at the cabin to tell him how it's going; hearing his voice would make this day even better. Our last conversation on Thursday evening wasn't quite long enough for me. The recorder comes on so I leave a message.

March 7, 1993 • Bill has not called back yet. I call the cabin and get the recorder again. Leave another message. Maybe he's gone back down to the house for a few days…. Call the house and leave a message on that recorder. I call the cabin one more time. Get the recorder again.

I pick up the messages. My message from yesterday is still on the tape. Where is he? I phone caretaker Jim.

While I wait on the phone, Jim looks across the lake at the cabin and tells me that the lights are on there. The message light on the recorder must not be working or Bill would have called me back. He tells me that he'll go over in the morning to let Bill know that I'm trying to reach him.

March 8, 1993 • A beautiful New Mexico Monday morning to begin my second week in training! At 10 A.M. we take our mid-morning break from class and I go to get Ciao to play. But instead of bounding out of the Jeep as usual, she's huddled against the back seat, unwilling to come out. I crawl in next to her and find that she's shaking like a leaf. We finally coax her out but she jumps right back in and won't come out.

I return to class reluctantly. At lunchtime, she's still in the same state. I look around for what might be upsetting her, but everything seems fine. My heart sinks at my inability to understand or help her. I go back in to call the vet.

Rachel calls me to the phone. It's Jim. He says something odd; he tells me that I'm strong. Why would he say that? His next words hit me like a hammer: "Bill took his life." What? He did what? WHAT!?

I am suddenly fetal on the floor, and a long time in the arms of Rachel, Rick, and my classmates. The world is swept away in a tsunami of tears. I just cry and cry and cry and cry and cry. Later, as Rick helps me walk to the meditation temple, a hawk circles above; its scream rips apart the fabric of my perfect life. I cannot speak. I do not know anything. We sit in silence, but the silence that was once a comfort now swallows me whole.

Later, my classmates walk out to the temple to sit with me. They each share their experiences while meditating in the classroom for Bill and me. Mounah, from Switzerland, gives me a piece of paper on which she has written her experience. She describes an image of a tall pole with brightly colored ribbons affixed to its tip, streaming out in all directions. I had received that very image in my session with the Higher Self last November when Bill and

I were here. After a long time sitting together, we walk back to the classroom. Rachel makes phone calls to Jim and my brother. She is the mother that I need right now.

March 9, 1993 • The reality of your final act pummels me, Bill. The usual six-hour flight home from Albuquerque to Grand Rapids takes twelve hours because the Midwest is being buried by a massive snowstorm. Buried, like me. On the layover in Minneapolis, it hits me that I will never see you again. Stumbling down the concourse, I cry like a pitiful orphan. People give me strange, sad, and scared looks. I'm too busy gasping at life's fierceness to care.

March 10, 1993 • Your body is being cremated. We met each other eight years ago today. Today. When we met, it was love, lust, and unrelenting pursuit of each other. Now, we're up in flames: you are burned out of existence and I am burned beyond recognition.

March 11, 1993 • I go to see your family. Everyone in the living room is cold and stony. No one moves to hug me or ask me how I am. The realization that they blame me for your death seeps slowly into my dulled brain. As I flee, a scapegoat runs alongside me.

THE FAILURE OF WORDS

She came and sat by me,
her thoughts loud in her head
beating down the air
like animals of sound.

I waited,
unable to touch by speech,
sensing
the impossibility.

Her uncertainty
was a palpable barrier
enclosing her.

Guarded by the watchdogs
of rejection
it held her prisoner,
her tongue heavy
with unsaid things.

I reached towards her
in my mind but,
denied tomorrow's wisdom,
"My dear" was all I said.

CHERRY EARLE,
NEW ZEALAND

March 12, 1993 • Art drives me to the funeral home to pick up your personal items and ashes in a manila envelope and cardboard box. In the car I hold your ashes in my lap; I'm surprised at how heavy they are. When we arrive at the cabin, Art asks me if I want him to come inside. I don't. This is mine to meet on my own.

It's cold and very still inside. A piece of paper is on the kitchen counter. You wrote my name and phone number in Santa Fe on it for whomever would find you. On the desk in the office are three neatly stacked folders. They are the files that you prepared for me to get through the legal and financial hell that you knew I would have to face. I blink in disbelief: you planned this like the executive that you were. God.

Neither the caretaker nor the sheriff found a note. I know that you left it where only I could find it.

March 15, 1993 • I am still searching for your note. Where did you leave it?

March 16, 1993 • I'm frantic. My tears fall into every drawer that I open to search for your note. Have you actually left without saying good-bye to me? There is a blizzard today. I walk across the lake and back. My sorrow is unbelievably overwhelming.

March 17, 1993 • I sleep in the loft instead of our bed and dream that you are walking down the road outside, away from the cabin—and away from me. Waves of grief gush through my lungs. My tears are endless and exhausting.

March 18, 1993 • After days of searching, I have to face the fact that you didn't say good-bye to me, in even the slightest way. I cannot believe it. Anger claws at my insides, trying to get at you. I can barely inhabit my body. I hate you for doing this.

March 19, 1993 • This evening I do what I have most resisted doing— opening the garage door. The BMW is parked next to the Jeep Wrangler.

The gas tanks in both are empty. The windows of the BMW are open. The driver's seat is reclined. I open the door and look in, still looking for you. Your jacket is in the back seat and your gloves are on the floor. You bought this car for me. Whatever was unspoken between us has disappeared into eternity, along with our future. I miss you beyond belief. How could you have done this to yourself—and to me?

March 20, 1993 • I struggle about whether to return to the training. I could just stay home, but that would be just another form of suicide, wouldn't it? The loons have taught me that it's either fly or die.

March 23, 1993 – May 7, 1993 • I return to Santa Fe. My classmates embrace my painful vulnerability with open arms and gentle counsel; they remind me about the loss of form, but never of Spirit. I know they are right, but it doesn't help to relieve the pain.

Rick and Rachel have purchased a tree that we plant near the temple. Thirteen of us gather in a circle around it and hold remembrance.

For the next three months I walk the path of my passion in a bottomless well of grief.

It is said that the greatest joy is born from the deepest sorrow. Well, I have to dive damn deep to find joy. Thankfully, I'm buoyed by the immense spiritual strength of Rick, Rachel, my classmates, and the other teachers in their willingness to equate my grief to a sacred process and give it a respected place within the training. The non-judgmental cornerstone of psycho-spiritual work and the hearts of my teachers and classmates embrace my horrendous process without flinching. This degree of spaciousness is a high teaching. I am among rare beings.

> First clean the inside of the teacup, so that the outside also may become clean.
> Matthew 23:26

The training carries on: energy healing modalities, Chinese medicine, Buddhist mindfulness and meditation practice, depth psychology, transpersonal states of consciousness, emotional healing, past life regression, and studies of world spiritual traditions, and more. My pain is mitigated by my absorption.

The most important purpose of the facilitator training is to heal within us the core theme of judgment/separation. As students and future facilitators, our task is to clear away the inner debris of our own negative tendencies. As for me, I must clear my themes of abandonment, betrayal, guilt, self-judgment, victim consciousness, and co-dependence to name just a few. Within this holistic modality of healing through the Higher Self, each session allows attachments and aversions to dissolve naturally as higher awareness take place. As my mental and emotional churnings, conflicts, and confusions unwind, I am liberated from lifelong patterns that have brought me only suffering. Rachel has given us a wonderful poem, author unknown, on letting go, which I need to read often:

> To let go does not mean to stop caring.
> It means that I can't do it for someone else.
> To let go is to not cut myself off.
> It's the realization that I can't control another.
> To let go is to not enable,
> but to allow learning from natural consequences.
> To let go is to admit powerlessness,
> which means the outcome is not in my hands.
> To let go is to not change or blame another,
> it's to make the most of myself.
> To let go is to not judge,
> but to allow another to be a human being.
> To let go is to not be in the middle,
> arranging all the outcome,
> but to allow others to arrange their own destinies.

To let go is to not be protective,
it's to permit another to face reality.
To let go is to not deny,
but to accept.
To let go is to not nag, scold or argue,
but to search out my own shortcomings
and correct them.
To let go is to not adjust everything to my desires,
but to try to take each day as it comes,
and to cherish my place in it.
To let go is to not criticize and regulate anybody,
but to try to become what I dream I can be.
To let go is to not regret the past,
but to grow and live for the future.
To let go is to fear less and live more.

In this time together we have become very close. Rick and Rachel have also provided us with equal opportunities for fun. In our group dinners and outings, as well as in class, laughter has been given a high priority.

May 13, 1993 • When you were forty years old, your girlfriend, Lucci, died in a car accident after a weekend with you at your cabin. I'm forty years old and it's you who has died in a car at our cabin. Our patterns pull us together by the vibration of their themes for only one reason— to heal them.

May 28, 1993 • I receive letters from people all over the world who knew and loved you. Some are written with sincere sympathy, but others barely hide blame and judgment. Without the foundation of strength that I've gained through this training and my inner work, I'd be dead from the daggers.

June 1, 1993 • I begin to see clients in Grand Rapids today. It's quite an experience to be both the wounded one and the healer. To hold a non-judgmental space for my clients as they seek wholeness is what it's all about. The wound I incurred at the start of my training was the door opener for the compassion I would need to serve others.

> There is a life force within your soul,
> seek that life.
> There is a gem in the mountain of
> your body, seek that mine.
> O traveler, if you are in search of That
> Don't look outside,
> look inside yourself and seek That.
>
> Jalaluddin Rumi

June 16, 1993 • The very things that held me to my family, your family, and the corporate family may well have been the things that held me back from my own life. Did it take this to get my own life to happen?

June 22, 1993 • As I kayak today, I watch the movement of the bugs on the surface of the water as choreography; chaotic movement is transformed into an intricate dance of unending turns, dips, and pirouettes. My vision is opening to allow me to either see chaos or choreography in whatever is happening in my life. I get to choose.

June 23, 1993 • Is loss a liability or is it liberation?

> The weak can never forgive.
> Forgiveness is the attribute
> of the strong.
> Mahatma Gandhi

June 21, 1993 • Forgiveness has abandoned me. Correction, I have abandoned forgiveness. There is a desert of anger in me and every grain of sand is still rubbing my insides raw. I know it's not fair to hold you hostage to my story. Still, I hate you for what you did.

June 29, 1993 • I walk the skin, muscles, and bones of the earth in the attempt to recover a rhythm, any rhythm, but grief insists on disorienting me—I keep getting lost in woods I know so well.

July 2, 1993 • I feel lost from soul, and I sit still to find it again.

July 6, 1993 • I fly up to Alaska with Dana and half of your ashes. After long talks with Chris in the last two months, I'm finally convinced that he and Marie will give her the life that she was born for. Life is giving me some unbelievably difficult choices to make.

July 7, 1993 • Tonight, Chris and I take Dana and his Lab by boat up the Copper River to your favorite fishing spot. We drink a bottle of French Bordeaux left for this occasion by Richard, one of your fishing buddies. I walk out to the middle of the river and drop your ashes and pocketknife into it. The current pulls them down and carries them away, yet I know they are still there in the river. As I look at that, I see life and death mingling with each other. The dogs play together. To them, everything's fine. And it is.

July 8, 1993 • Chris takes me to where you and he used to fish for grayling. I nestle your watch into the rocks. I'm exhausted.

July 11, 1993 • Dana follows us down to the beach as Chris loads my gear into the floatplane to fly from the lodge to Iliamna to catch my flight back to Anchorage. When she realizes that I'm in the plane and she's not, Dana plunges into the water and swims frantically toward the plane as Chris pulls it away from the dock. I'm abandoning my dog. I'm abandoning your dog. I weep ceaselessly all the way to Iliamna and all the way to Anchorage. What were you thinking when you left me behind?

July 14, 1993 • Today I get lost in the grocery store. Unbelievable.

July 15, 1993 • Kathy, Bill's ex-wife, drives up to the cabin to visit me today. She shows me a four-page legal document that Bill's sister had shared

> One going to take a pointed stick to pinch a baby bird should first try it on himself to feel how it hurts.
> Yoruba Proverb (Nigeria)

with her last week. Bill's family had hired an attorney, the father of the best man at our wedding no less, to attempt to find our marriage "non-binding," thus giving them grounds to contest the will and get the money in the estate. As stated in the will, all assets went to me, of course. I guess they couldn't handle the fact that he'd left no money to them. This isn't surprising. It's going to take them a while to get used to no more free lunches—the family benefactor has left town and I'm the one left to get mad at. Now I know where the sharp pain between my shoulder blades is coming from.

July 17, 1993 • Grief grabs at me today as I box up your life. I take your Armani suits to the community shelter. You ended your life as homeless as the homeless who will now wear your clothes.

July 23, 1993 • Tonight at 8:30 the moon is rising as I kayak across the big lake. There is little breeze left, leaving the surface smooth, allowing effortless paddling. I remind myself to be quiet, even in my breathing. I call to Spirit. Suddenly, a great horned owl flies directly over my head in the direction I am going. A whippoorwill calls from the woods at the edge of the lake. One of the loons glides less than ten feet off the bow of the kayak, seemingly oblivious to it. My heart starts to pound. Something's up.

> Not one of you is a believer until he loves for his brother what he loves for himself.
> Islam. Number 13 of Imam "Al-Nawawi's Forty Hadiths"

It's dark by the time I arrive at the opposite shore. I turn right past the loon island, listening my way along the shore, following it by the rustle of the grasses close to me. Then I hear a strange sound, like bubbles being blown in the water. I stop paddling and let the kayak slide silently. A deer drinking at the shore? Suddenly, the shiny wet body of an otter glides across a narrow sliver of moonlight on the water. I can feel the vibration of its breath as it swims right next to the kayak. There are more. The otter and its mates are feeding on crayfish in the submerged weeds. Why don't they swim away from me? For God's sake, don't they see me? Am I invisible? I hold my breath. They swim and dive all around my boat, which is held still by the reeds. After a few precious, but breathless minutes, the wind shifts, gently pulling me away from them. I will never be the same again. God.

August 7, 1993 • Tonight, the fireflies light up the woods like flying fairies. As I walk in their midst, I feel keenly like them, my own light blinking on and off —joy, sorrow, joy, sorrow.

August 9, 1993 • One of Bill's "friends" at the Club, with a snoot full of booze comes over to the cabin with his consolation mask in place. After a few minutes it slips to reveal his motive. Oh man, why this? I'm being preyed upon for money and sex. If it's not the financial planners, it's the next-door neighbor. My tour of the underbelly of human nature continues. Yuck.

Power-lust is a weed that grows only in the vacant lot of an empty mind.
Ayn Rand

October 9, 1993 • I find an old, shed snakeskin on a log near the channel. I know what I've outgrown and it's most of myself. It's a good thing I no longer enjoy keeping old clothes in my closet.

There's one young loon left on the lake; its parents and twin have flown to wintering grounds. It swims close to the bow of my kayak as if it knows me. I float alone, too. Just as I am wondering what is next in life for me, it suddenly turns toward me, stretches out its wings and pulls its body upward. There I am in the loon's mirror, stretching my wings as I get ready to fly!

I am facilitating people from all walks of life in gaining a conscious connection to their Higher Self. I am fortunate to witness Spirit's love.

November 6, 1993 • I am happy to see that the young loon has found the wind and is on its way to wintering grounds. Quite a contrast to last year's young one, succumbing to death because it was unable to fly. Life was mirroring Bill's death in that loon's fate…and I never saw it.

December 12, 1993 • I go to the Point to listen. All is quiet as I walk the path along the river. Water playing music over rocks and through partially submerged branches of fallen trees. Fall? You? It never occurred to me that you could even so much as stumble. I just couldn't discern the demons that were devouring you. As I step into the clearing, crows circle overhead, calling. I watch them, waiting for a message. Then, an eagle appears. Let me see, please let me be able to see.

December 14, 1993 • My tortured steps now seem to be scribing a perfect path. Through my Higher Self, heaven has emerged from hell.

December 16, 1993

> Let me not pray to be sheltered from dangers
> But to be fearless in facing them
> Let me not beg for the stilling of my pain
> But for the heart to conquer it.
> Let me not crave in anxious fear to be saved
> but hope for the patience
> to win my freedom.

Rabindranath Tagore

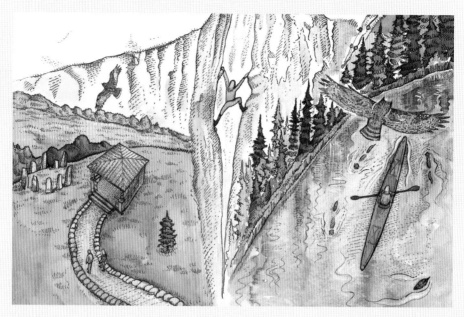

Sherpa Norbu's Parable

I study Shaypa's steps as she crosses the icefall. She is trekking with an unnerving lack of awareness. She doesn't even notice the bodies of the dead and injured that we pass. Their predicaments reveal the consequences of past choices. I can tell that she has yet to recognize the lessons that they are there to teach.

I try to warn her of the dangers that exist on this part of the mountain; the ice and snow are constantly shifting or giving way underfoot. One never knows where the next crevasse will be. If she only knew that every footprint she places in the present will appear in her future. But she's too smug to hear me.

Then it happens. A snow bridge collapses underneath her. A sudden rush of air, charged with an enormous and impersonal force, pulls her down into the icy abyss.

Shaypa plummets downward, crashing against unforgiving walls of ice, flailing helplessly as she disappears into the narrow, frozen cavern.

Down here it's so quiet that she can hear her own thoughts. The panoramas of past life choices replay in her mind, much as they do at the moment of death. Shaypa hears for the first time the murky motives that spawned many of her life choices. This is painful. Is this pain what has kept her from listening to her thoughts while she was thinking them? Shaypa now realizes why she has never been a good listener.

The light in the crevasse is dimmed by the depth of her fall. She can no longer see or hear me. The walls of ice above her offer nothing for escape. Though it doesn't make sense to her, Shaypa realizes with frightened urgency that she must descend in order to find her way out to the opening above.

Looking downward she notices that the walls are jagged, offering her hand and footholds. Even though it is extremely cold in the cavern, she sweats with the effort and care that it takes to avoid falling. Shaypa knows that is imperative that she remains awake and aware for every move—but that is easier said than done. Despair has descended with her. Frightening thoughts occur to her: might she never find her way out and might she never find me?

She feels it in her hands first. They ache from gripping the serrated ice so tightly. Shaypa looks frantically over her shoulder into the abyss below. "I will surely die in this freezing hot hell," she cries pitifully, her breath shallow and labored. Then she realizes that her hands aren't gripping the ice rungs at all, but that she is actually gripping her own throat! Shaypa is choking the life out of herself, and it is fear that fuels her grip!

My last teaching to her about interconnection with others returns as a pang in her solar plexus. She hasn't understood it until now.

"If I am choking myself with fear, is my fear also choking others?" It is the darkest thought Shaypa has ever had. She knows that she must somehow release the stranglehold she has on herself—and on everyone and everything in her life.

"The fear in my hands is actually the fear in my mind that seeks control. The need to control is really fear in disguise! When I control others, fear is actually controlling me. When I manipulate others, fear is actually manipulating me. When I control others to win, I am really the loser. Oh, Norbu, I have fallen into the crevasse of my own mind!" Shaypa wails bleakly.

"So, where is love in all this?"

Startled, Shaypa looks up toward the opening.

"Norbu, I realize now that my motives have created this crevasse!" she shouts up from the darkness.

In the very next instant, Shaypa reappears on the icefall beside me.

"Shaypa, it takes courage to change. But the source of your power to do just that is always there to help you," I advise her. "And remember, your life is in your heart as well as your hands. It's all in the way that you use them."

Shaypa opens her hands and watches in amazement as her heart drops like a feather into them.

"Fear lives in closed hearts and closed hands," I tell her. "When your heart is open, your hands will be open. Keep both open to receive love from life—and life from love."

Next to me stands a tall pole anchored in the snow. Countless ribbons of every color flutter outward in all directions from the top of the pole. With the brightly colored sungdhi tied around my neck, I, Norbu Sherpa, look like the pole. Shaypa curiously regards the ribbons flowing freely in all directions from the poles apex.

"The point at the top of the pole where each ribbon is attached is the Source," I explain. When you make a true connection with the Source, all for the good proceeds from there."

Shaypa touches the sungdhi that is looped around her neck to remind herself that she is, and always will be, one of those ribbons. And with that, we turn toward higher ground and begin to walk again.

New Spring

Dear love,
The world we knew
is composting,
breaking down,
decomposing those beliefs
that grew like weeds
among the blossoms of the past.

Some cosmic gardener
is raking the scattered leaves
of thoughtlessness,
the chickweed of greed,
and catching up
the deadwood of hate,
to fling upon the smouldering pile.

Poor warring earth,
heated by emotion
loosed in anger of those
yesterdays,
that gave today its birth.
Choked with couch weed and bramble
is the garden
we ever seek to make.

Now from every corner
can we take the dying atoms
of belief,
to reincarnate?
Can we, like spring,
create again in beauty,
in the rich black loam
still germinate
and spring to bloom…
to change our living ways?

Cherry Earle, New Zealand

CRISIS OF CLARITY

Timeless Values Travel Well

THE TERRITORY

The quality of being clear in what you are thinking or expressing

YOUR APPROXIMATE AGE

North Travel Group	(1936-1946)	41
South Travel Group	(1947-1957)	41
East Travel Group	(1958-1968)	40
West Travel Group	(1969-1979)	40

TIME IN TRANSIT

Two years

WHAT TO PACK OR ACQUIRE ALONG THE WAY

Physical:	Health
Mental:	Discrimination and Discernment
Emotional:	Stability
Spiritual:	Inspiration

WHAT TO LEAVE BEHIND

The rose-colored glasses

THE WEATHER FORECAST

Dense fog

THE MANTRA

Nothing is as it seems to be.

TRAVEL ITINERARY

During the Crisis of Clarity, a period of approximately two years, you will be meeting challenges that are intended to help you determine what you can realistically accomplish from this time forward and to help you identify those values you will need in order to steward your higher life purpose.

Upon entering the Crisis of Clarity, you may think that you have a pretty good idea of who you are—but the experiences you have during this crisis may teach you differently. Events that happen during the Crisis of Clarity are meant to help you separate fact from fiction.

Beware: this part of the journey is fogbound. As much as you might try to navigate certain experiences with your eyes and ears open, your ability for clear perception may be elusive or absent.

During this crisis, specific experiences will expose your illusions and self-deceptions. But by practicing discernment and discrimination, you will become less subject to future deceptions or disappointments to which rose-colored glasses make you susceptible. By the end of this crisis, you will be able to regard individuals and situations for whom and what they really are, rather than what you thought or hoped they could or would be.

Seemingly significant ideas may arise during this crisis and, as much as you might like to believe right now, not all of them will be practical for your life. If certain goals, relationships, careers, or other aspects of your life dissolve during this time, trust that you are being guided to those better suited to your higher life purpose. Strive to stay realistic.

By their actions, other people will help you to define your values. Which values do you need to incorporate into your life in order to "beautify" it?

By your actions, you may be the one who helps others define their value systems. What values are you modeling for others to incorporate into their lives?

Above all, don't despair about any failed dreams! If you follow the rules of the road, clarity will emerge, but most likely not until at, or shortly after, the conclusion of this crisis. Then, you will be able to make better decisions from what you have learned about yourself and others. And by successfully parting ways with your rose-colored glasses, you will acquire a trustworthy foundation of values from which to live and thrive.

ESSENTIAL TRAVEL TIPS

- Avoid fantasies, but safeguard your dreams.
- Practice non-attachment, but keep your heart open.
- Honor your imagination by giving it an honored place in your life.
- Discover transcendence, but don't use it to escape.
- Use your intuition in concert with your intellect.
- Call upon objective parties to help you analyze important situations or decisions.
- Avoid making permanent commitments until the conclusion of this crisis. By doing so you can avoid having to live with the consequences of ill-conceived ideas or erroneous perceptions that are common to this crisis.

Ultimate Travel Tip:

Keep your truth and beauty detector tuned up at all times.

If truth is beauty how come nobody has their hair done in the library?

Lily Tomlin

SIGHTS AND SOUNDS

This is a list of the kinds of things that you may find along the way through the Crisis of Clarity. You can recognize these as personal traits or as symbolic messages in your dreams. You are free to choose which can be of real and lasting help for the rest of your journey.

Addiction
Aesthetics
Alienation
Ambiguity
Anemia
Angels
Art
Assumption
Betrayal
Blind spots
Bliss
Boats
Camouflage
Charity
Cinema
Clairvoyants
Clarity
Clouds
Compassion
Con artists
Confession
Confusion
Counselors
Deception
Devotion
Discernment
Discouragement

Disappointment
Discrimination
Dishonesty
Disillusionment
Disloyalty
Distortion
Divinity
Doubt
Dreams
Drifting
Drowning
Drugs
Ecstasy
Enigma
Escapism
Fakes
Fantasies
Fascination
Floods
Fog
Fraud
Gratitude
Gullibility
Gurus
Honesty
Hypersensitivity
Hypnosis

Hypochondria
Hypocrisy
Hysteria
Idealism
Illusion
Imagination
Impersonators
Impracticality
Infatuation
Inferiority
   complex
Inspiration
Instability
Intuition
Investigators
Leaks
Lethargy
Magic
Meaninglessness
Melodrama
Misrepresentation
Missionaries
Music
Mystery
Mystics
Mythology
Neurosis

Non-attachment
Oceans
Oil
Parables
Paranoia
Photography
Plumbers
Psychic receptivity
Refinement
Religious devotion
Retreats
Reverence
Savior/victim/
   martyr scenarios
Selflessness
Scandal
Seclusion
Secrets
Seduction
Ships
Spiritual
   advancement
Uncertainty
Utopianism
Vacillation
Visions
Wanderlust
Water

Traveling Companions

Mother Teresa, India

Mother Teresa opened Nirmal Hriday (Pure Heart), Home for Dying Destitutes. It was here that Indians, who were dying in the streets of Calcutta, could die in peace and dignity under the care of the Sisters of Charity.

Marie, France

Marie met a man and quickly became infatuated with him. He was everything she thought she wanted in a partner. "We were married for five years until I found out that he had a girlfriend the entire time he was with me. I took off my rose-colored glasses and divorced him."

Paul, Australia

"I hadn't played the piano for over twenty years," says Paul. "I had lost touch with myself and my music to a frenetic career in finance."

"I hired a pianist to entertain guests at my party. That evening when he took a break, I nervously edged my way to the piano and sat down. As my fingers touched the keyboard, the music seemed to flow from the piano into my soul, reawakening me to the joy that had lain dormant and forgotten in my heart for so many years. After that, I made time every day to play the piano and, believe it or not, I became happier in my job!"

Gerhard, Germany

Gerhard decided to take a short sabbatical from his work as a librarian and rented a secluded cabin in the woods for some time alone.

"One morning, I awoke with an idea that was both surprising and compelling." Over the next three days he "received by inspiration" the concept for a documentary film.

"The experience was like being swept down an internal river of inspiration," Gerhard recalls. "All I had to do was hold out my hands and catch ideas and images as they flowed by." He acted on his inspiration by producing the film, and when it debuted, it was met with wide acclaim.

KETUT, INDONESIA

Ketut was approached by a co-worker who told him of an opportunity to obtain a job on a cruise ship sailing out of Jakarta. The salary would be eight times more than his current income. Having difficulty paying for his sons' school tuition, Ketut jumped at the chance to improve his children's educational prospects.

In order to qualify for the job, he had to travel to Jakarta, obtain a passport, and pay one million rupia for "training." He was then told to return home and wait to be called for the job on the cruise ship. He never received the call. Ketut lost not only his one million rupia but also his old job, which he had already quit to take the new one.

SUSAN, UNITED STATES

It was late October and the weather was rainy with dense fog when Susan picked up her daughter from after-school band practice. A short distance from home, she made a right turn onto what she thought was the correct road. Susan and her daughter drowned in their car in thirteen feet of water after driving off a boat ramp at the end of the road.

JOHN, ENGLAND

John, a photojournalist, filmed a powerful documentary tracing the methamphetamine drug trade from Asia to Great Britain. It increased public awareness of the tendency of the drug to foster violence in young people.

It's not hard to make decisions when you know what your values are.

Roy Disney

BUDDHISM

HAWAIIAN HUNA

McKenzie's Journal

December 17, 1993 • Patty calls me tonight to tell me that if she doesn't have sixty thousand dollars by Monday she will be forced to declare bankruptcy in her business. She asks for a thirty-day bridge loan. How can I refuse my own sister?

February 3, 1994 • Patty's having a difficult time repaying the loan. I feel for her: she worked so hard to build her business only to have it end up like this.

March 1, 1994 • Ciao and I leave Santa Fe for the cabin earlier than usual so that we can watch spring arrive after the snow departs. Lots of fires to sit and read by. Still good snowshoeing. And I get to listen to the ice crack and groan as it shifts under the spring sun.

March 4, 1994 • I fly down to Chicago for a workshop taught by Dr. Gay Luce. Several other people from the Midwest also attend. We learn about healing practices originating from some of the indigenous traditions. On Sunday afternoon, I meet with Gay to discuss attending her Nine Gates Mystery School in California.

March 7, 1994 • I'm anxious to go to Nine Gates Mystery School. I'm not sure what it will be exactly, but I feel a responsibility to continue to enlarge myself and deepen my spiritual life. It will also add another dimension to what I can offer of myself to my clients. How essential it is that I never stop learning (mostly about myself) so that I can become a teacher in the truest sense of the word.

In my dream, the angel shrugged and said, "If we fail this time it will be a failure of imagination," and then she placed the world gently in the palm of my hand.

From "Imagining World", by Brian Andreas

April 22 – May 1, 1994 • In San Francisco for Part I of Nine Gates Mystery School! The purpose of the next nine days is, through Celtic, Native American, and Sufi teachings, to strengthen our connection to the Earth, build trust and community, work with subtle healing energies, explore ego, emotions, and individual will, and open the heart center to compassion and joy. There are thirty-six of us in the class, representing many faith traditions. It's exciting to be with all of these people, just like it was to have met people of many cultures in my travels with Bill.

Through this spiritual work I commit to seeing that all of my life experiences are lived in service to others. This is the evolutionary journey I have chosen.

May 2, 1994 • Now in a cat-and-mouse game with Patty. I'm spending my time chasing her and she's dodging me in every way she can. Not fun. And this is my sister?

I kayak a short distance from the shore this evening so I don't interrupt the symphony of spring peepers.

May 17, 1994 • Grand Rapids is no longer my place. My old friendships have fallen away. Santa Fe is where I need to go to live the life that is true for me.

June 21, 1994 • I drive to Grand Rapids to visit Diane today. Her last bone scan shows that the cancer has moved into her lower vertebrae and right hip. It's ironic that someone so sick can be such a touchstone, inspiration, and ballast for me. She shows me how to live in another way.

I love her.

June 27, 1994 • The light is long and luxurious these days. The loon chicks are growing quickly. The herons are fishing the shoreline. The different species of birds combine their songs in the woods. Cabin life teaches me what beauty is.

July 19, 1994 • Around the issue of the money lent to Patty: the mess continues. I hire an attorney to track her down. Sixty thousand dollars is a lot of money. I'm sick about this! Mostly, I am unbelievably disappointed in myself. I thought I was a pretty smart person up until now.

August 1, 1994 • I kayak this evening while Ciao runs the path around the lake, occasionally splashing chest high along the shoreline. We are joined at the hip, this dog and I.

August 5-10, 1994 • Fly to Santa Fe to look for a house to buy and find one. Thrilled. This means, though, that I won't be able to be at the cabin as much as before. Not so thrilled. Sacrifice time. How can I do Santa Fe for me and the cabin for both Ciao and me?

September 23, 1994 • Part II of Nine Gates Mystery School begins today here in Ojai, California. We will study the spiritual traditions of Hinduism, esoteric Christianity, Hawaiian Huna, and Tibetan Buddhism, learn to communicate with clarity and honesty, practice Hindu chant, deepen the intuition, learn how to see death as a gateway, and deepen appreciation of the transcendent realms. These practices are not, by any means, an intellectual overview, but direct experience with each. I am HOME!

October 11, 1994 • Move into the Santa Fe house. Can't believe I'm here. Mountains all around me. Good little Capricorn.

October 15, 1994 • Return to the cabin to spend the last days of fall in the woods and tie up loose ends, like my sister issue—ugh.

October 18, 1994 • Patty still evading me. I just can't believe that my own sister would do this!

October 30, 1994 • This morning Ciao and I sit on the dock and say good-bye to the woods, water, and all the creatures. A veil-like mist drifts across the lake, slowly dissipating as the sun filters through the oaks, maples, and cedars circling the shore. She and I migrating to Santa Fe like two birds obeying the seasonal shift.

January 5, 1994 • I take Ciao up to Wilderness Gate for a walk. A twelve-acre lot has come up for sale at the back of the development. Wow, here's an opportunity to actually live in our favorite hiking place. I mentally construct a house and a horse barn.

January 7, 1994 • I contact the owner of the lot. The price is ridiculously expensive. That's Santa Fe.

January 18, 1995 • Walk the Wilderness Gate property again today with Ciao; wow, what it'll be like to live on a mountain with pinions and ponderosas around me.

February 21, 1995 • After a lot of back and forth, Rob, the property owner, and I reach an agreement on a price. This is just fantastic!

March 19, 1995 • I'm at Santa Fe Title Company for the Wilderness Gate property closing today. While I'm writing the check for the deposit, the closing officer advises me that Rob is currently being sued for easement rights for a road that would run right next to my lot. That road and the traffic on it would ruin my reasons for living there—namely peace, quiet, and solitude. It would also cut the property value in half, literally. Rob should have disclosed this, but he didn't. I feel like I've been hit with a baseball bat. No, I have been hit with a baseball bat. And I'm livid beyond belief.

March 29, 1995 • I am still working through both my anger and disappointment about Wilderness Gate; miserable about all the time and energy I spent to have it come to nothing. I'm even more miserable because I don't understand why this has happened.

April 1, 1995 • Patty is still dodging me and I'm still in shock that my own sister would do this. I do a Higher Self session to untangle my knots of confusion. It certainly is April Fool's Day.

> There is only one thing more painful than learning from experience, and that is not learning from experience.
> Laurens van der Post

April 2, 1995 • In yesterday's session I find the roots of my gullibility. I have to learn how to be more discriminating and discerning. This will take practice.

April 14, 1995 • Ciao and I fly home for the summer. Diane is back in the hospital, this time on morphine. For the first two weeks I drive back and forth from the cabin to Grand Rapids to sit with her. I notice how intimacy grows in the most challenging conditions.

April 15, 1995 • Bill would have turned fifty-three today. At the Point, I make a fire at the foot of the Three Sisters and burn some of the photographs of our life together. Watching them melt in the flames, I see the co-dependent co-conspiracy that was there to teach me what love is and what love is not. Was Bill a wonderful man? Yes. Is Patty a child of God? Sure. But the memory and metaphor of my first job of pulling near-drowning victims from the pool, as a Chicago lifeguard, is no longer lost on me. From now on, pull them out of the water, but ask them if they're willing to learn how to swim. And hear their answers by their actions!

Sherpa Norbu's Parable

I sit before my altar in the yurt, eyes closed, my breath moving me deeper into my morning meditation. Soon, the crown of my head begins to burn with familiar divine heat and, with my inner eye, I watch the objects on my altar slowly fade.

Then, as easily as I lose myself to the unity of all things, I return to my place before the altar. I open my eyes to see that everything is just as it was before. Giving each knee a slight squeeze, I slowly rise and bow in gratitude for the moment of remembrance.

Pushing back the door flap, I peer out. A mist has settled over the shoulders of the mountain. It is so impenetrable that I cannot see my hand at the end of my outstretched arm.

At the opposite end of camp Shaypa has difficulty waking up. Lingering on her cot, she groggily recalls a dream about the blue sky above the summit. She crawls out of her tent into the same heavy mist. With a sleepy sigh, she looks for her boots that have disappeared in fog. I call to her, but Shaypa, still trying to locate her boots, does not hear me.

"I can't see a thing," she grumbles to herself.

She creeps tentatively toward what she thinks will be the center of camp. Prayer flags strung between the tents flutter back and forth like mirages, appearing and disappearing in the mist. Rocks and bushes advance toward her like hungry ghosts. She turns to avoid them, but is too late. Scraped and bruised, Shaypa is perplexed.

"How could I not have seen those bushes? I knew exactly where they were yesterday!" she protests. Shaypa realizes nervously that she has lost her bearings. "Nothing is as it seems to be in this terrain!"

She anxiously reassesses her orienteering skills. Casting her eyes back and forth as she continues her creep over the rocks, she finds that she still fails to see anything until she has stumbled into it.

"I can't see the path!" Shaypa's senses spin like a confused compass and she is disappointed in herself for losing her sense of direction. The path is all-important to Shaypa, for she believes that it is her duty to know where it is at all times. Now completely disoriented and frightened to make another move, she sits for what seems a very long time, chastising herself for her predicament.

"Shaypa!" I call into the thick fog.

"Norbu, where are you!" Shaypa is hugely relieved to hear my voice, distant though it still is.

"I am here, in the fog."

"Where? Where?" implores Shaypa.

"I am in the fog, Shaypa."

"What can I do?" she asks.

"Find me" I reply. "Stumble if you will, but find me."

Shaypa inches toward my voice.

"I still can't see you," she complains.

"I am here. Listen inwardly and you will find me."

"Norbu, how long will this fog delay us? I want to get back onto the path. I want to see the blue sky above the summit that I dreamed of this morning."

I know how unhappy Shaypa is with these uncertain conditions. I know that Shaypa doesn't yet realize that the mountain presents all climbers with the fog at this stage of their ascent for a very good reason.

"This fog will persist as long as it must," I reply with an equanimity that annoys Shaypa.

When Shaypa finally recognizes her aversion to uncertainty, she notices that the condensing mist has immersed her from head to toe.

"Ah-ha!" Shaypa cries in a sudden flash of relief. "The fog that seemingly plagues me, in fact, bathes me!"

Shaypa realizes that uncertainty is a compassionate teacher on this part of the mountain. Too much certainty has made her senses lazy and her steps slipshod. But my voice in the fog has saved her from walking off the side of the mountain.

Gently, I lift Shaypa's chin to meet my gaze directly. In my eyes she can now see what they have reflected all along—the breathtaking beauty of the brilliant blue sky above the summit.

Dream Life

Alone she sleeps
and yet
is not alone.
In her dreaming
the bonds of flesh dissolve
and melt away,
bringing to her
vast horizons of life,
past and future,
with other loves,
and people now unknown.

She weeps
in the sorrow
of her memories
that become again her now;
feels the deep joys
of tomorrow's loves;
travels in a breath
the wind cool space of time.
Alone she sleeps,
her other days beside her, waiting to be lived.

CHERRY EARLE, NEW ZEALAND

CRISIS OF STATURE

Integrity has Deep Roots

THE TERRITORY

Development, growth, or level of attainment, especially
as worthy of high regard

YOUR APPROXIMATE AGE

North Travel Group	(1936-1946)	42-44
South Travel Group	(1947-1957)	45-43
East Travel Group	(1958-1968)	44-42
West Travel Group	(1969-1979)	42-45

TIME IN TRANSIT

Up to one year

WHAT TO PACK OR ACQUIRE ALONG THE WAY

Physical:	Resilience
Mental:	Fortitude
Emotional:	Stability
Spiritual:	Discipline

WHAT TO LEAVE BEHIND

Self-doubt

THE WEATHER FORECAST

Chance of storms

THE MANTRA

Missed steps are missteps.

TRAVEL ITINERARY

When a tree is well rooted, it is far less likely to be blown over during storms. During the Crisis of Stature, your strength, maturity, depth, integrity, and self-discipline will be tested.

The Crisis of Stature will require your willingness to:

- Stand strong in the face of challenges to your principles.
- Take ownership of both your successes and failures.
- Maintain high principles and professional standards.
- Shun shortcuts, because missed steps will require backtracking at some inconvenient time in the future, resulting in lost time and opportunity.
- Share the knowledge and wisdom of your experience.

During this crisis, certain elements of your life may cease working and you may experience a breakdown of certain activities and/or relationships. This may be accompanied by a sense of emptiness, futility or failure, bitterness, resentment, or doubt. If you encounter difficulties, it is not time to stop or turn back. It is simply necessary to restructure your life to find the path on which you can re-energize your passion and live strong from your acquired cache of wisdom.

If your life is flourishing and you are having good results, feel good that you have learned how to align mind, heart, and action. Then, share your stature by helping others to achieve theirs!

ESSENTIAL TRAVEL TIPS

- Eliminate from your life that which is outworn, irrelevant, or inefficient.

- Consolidate your activities to strengthen to the best of them.

- Discover how to recombine the best parts of yourself to create something useful. This will renew your energy and enthusiasm.

- Incorporate into your relationships and activities more dimension and perspective and invite others to participate. This requires more responsibility, but increases your personal effectiveness.

The Ultimate Travel Tip:

Short cuts don't lead anywhere worth going.

We have the Bill of Rights. What we need is a Bill of Responsibilities.

Bill Maher

SIGHTS AND SOUNDS

This is a list of the kinds of things that you may find along the way through the Crisis of Stature. You can recognize these as personal traits or as symbolic messages in your dreams. You are free to choose which of these can be of real and lasting value for the rest of your life journey.

Accountability	Cowards	Impenetrability	Reduction
Aloofness	Cynics	Indispensability	Reliability
Ambition	Debts	Inertia	Resentment
Animosity	Defeat	Inflexibility	Resistance
Anxiety	Deliberation	Integrity	Responsibilities
Apathy	Demotion	Intolerance	Restraints
Apprehension	Despair	Introspection	Restrictions
Asceticism	Diligence	Isolation	Retreats
Ashes	Discipline	Loneliness	Rigidity
Austerity	Discretion	Losses	Seclusion
Aversion	Dissatisfaction	Melancholy	Self-confidence
Bankruptcy	Doubt	Narrow-mindedness	Self-control
Bitterness	Efficiency	Obstructions	Simplicity
Bones	Elders	Oppression	Skepticism
Boredom	Endurance	Orderliness	Sobriety
Brevity	Failures	Patience	Steadfastness
Burdens	Fatigue	Permanence	Stoicism
Calm	Fear	Perseverance	Stubbornness
Caution	Fortitude	Persistence	Tediousness
Chiropractors	Foundations	Pessimism	Tenacity
Common sense	Frugality	Poise	Thoroughness
Concentration	Frustration	Practicality	Thrift
Conciseness	Fundamentals	Precision	Tranquility
Condemnation	Guilt	Principles	Trees (old)
Conservativeness	Hindsight	Prudence	Wisdom
Consolidation	Hoarding	Realism	Work
Contractions	Humility	Reason	Worry

TRAVELING COMPANIONS

MOTHER TERESA, INDIA

Local and international acknowledgements began to honor the accomplishments of the Sisters of Charity.

A.J., UNITED STATES

After suffering her fourth miscarriage and the loss of her beloved dog, Scooby, A.J. developed severe panic disorder and agoraphobia. Despite her long-standing role as a dynamic therapist who used her dogs in animal assisted therapy for hospital patients and nursing home residents, A.J. became unable to leave her house. It was now A.J. who needed a service dog to lead her back into the world. Unfortunately, her new dog, Sparky, had recently become aggressive and therefore unsuitable for the role.

A.J. called Cesar Milan, founder of the Dog Psychology Center in Los Angeles. Applying his expertise and experience, Cesar worked with both A.J. and Sparky, teaching them the skills they would need to pass the service dog certification testing—and they passed with flying colors! During the many hours spent working with Cesar, A.J. was able to reclaim the personal authority and skills that had been lost to her agoraphobia.

Since the airing of *The Dog Whisperer* television show featuring A.J.'s and Sparky's journey back onto the path of their higher life purpose, A.J.'s life has dramatically changed. "Admitting I had a mental disability on national television made it impossible for me to go back to living the way I was," she recalls.

Because of A.J.'s courage and perseverance, countless individuals living with panic disorder were inspired to get help for themselves. She and Sparky attended the Voice Awards, an event that recognizes people in the media who portray mental illness accurately. She was invited to appear with Sparky in the film, *Point of View: A Dogumentary*, which was a finalist at the Student Academy Awards in California. Sparky was chosen to star in the Hallmark movie, *A Kiss at Midnight*.

McKenzie's Journal

January 8, 1998 • I drive up to Leelanau County to look for real estate—trying to find my place for the long-term future. Recent dreams of sidewalks and crowds making me feel crowded. Return to the cabin having found nothing.

February 12, 1998 • Today I ski through snow-white woods, grateful to be alone on seven hundred pristine acres. I have skied the two-track halfway around the property when three men on snowmobiles roar up behind me. Only trespassers wouldn't know that the Club's rules prohibit recreational vehicles. But it's not trespassers—it's the president of the Club himself, sneaking his downstate friends for a little joy ride through our woods in the middle of the week when he thought nobody would be around to catch him. He tries to drive his snowmobile around me but I block him, daring him.

February 13, 1998 • I write a letter to the membership to describe the incident, calling for the president's resignation.

March 6, 1998 • My horse, Nell, turns four years old today. The thoroughbred and quarter horse in her are blooming!

April 3, 1998 • Today Ciao is eleven years old. I follow her across the river, up and down embankments, across the river again…and again. After two hours I'm exhausted and she's not. Joy and endorphins have diminished her hip pain.

April 21, 1998 • I've heard back from only two of the eleven members on the snowmobile issue. My indignation about the damn snowmobiles trashing the woods is sideswiped by their complacency. Nine members out of eleven don't have the backbone to stand up for the Club's own conservation ethic. Wow.

April 26, 1998 • Tonight I walk the path around the little lake in the dark. My feet find the way for me.

May 21, 1998 • I sit in meditation, remembering Diane's death one year ago today. The full moon that night was in the sign of Scorpio. At the cabin, I sat on the living room floor in the dark watching the moon's round, white, feminine face rise slowly over the lake. The phone had rung a little after 9:00 P.M. It was Jim, telling me that Diane had just passed over. My friend was born under a full moon in the sign of Scorpio on December 8, 1949. She had chosen the night of this same Scorpio moon to pass away. The perfect timing of events is always there. And always evident to those who know where to look.

May 31, 1998 • I float in the kayak this evening to listen to the whirr of spring peepers. I can't discern the beginnings nor endings in their music, probably because births and deaths, arrivals and departures are one symphony playing without beginning or end. Diane comes to mind again. I miss her so.

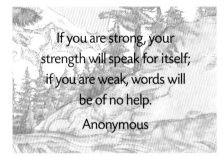

If you are strong, your strength will speak for itself; if you are weak, words will be of no help.

Anonymous

June 6, 1998 • I run into Jill and Kathleen, two of my clients, at the bookstore. They tell me how much their inner work is helping them to stay centered and peaceful. My own work—to heal the core judgment themes in myself is what provides the non-judgmental presence for others as they clear their own themes. This is why healers, myself included, must heal themselves first, last, and always.

June 18, 1998 • Today I plant shallots, eggplant, tomatoes, and basil. Tonight I kayak to watch the setting sun be overtaken by an approaching storm, but not before it gets the chance to illuminate the raindrops.

My work with clients is busy—very busy. In fact, it has become a revolving door. Every day brings more opportunities to witness flawless divine design and perfect timing. I've acquired ability for synthesis and an intuitive comprehension of complex patterns.

I still marvel at how the spontaneous appearance of archetypes in the psyche provides self-correction for inner conflict and confusion. Through the influence of conscious contact with the Higher Self, inner masculine and feminine energies come into balance so automatically. When yin and yang are in balance, good things happen for people!

June 26, 1998 • Life is full. There is a quiet joy in me now that is constant amidst the upheavals of the last few years. I also think how much Ciao has weathered with me. All I want to do is find ways to make life better for her. I could not have a better friend right now with whom to share mornings on the dock, Jeep rides, and the Point.

June 27, 1998 • The Club president, still incensed that I exposed his snowmobile trespass to the membership last winter, shows up at my cabin to pick a fight. I meet him face-to-face without returning anger. This is a very different way for me to be. I've learned that reactionary emotions weaken me. He's infuriated that he can't intimidate me. There is nothing to defend except the wildness of these woods, and that I will do.

June 28, 1998 • I write and submit a new bylaw, to be considered at the Club's annual meeting in September, which would prohibit the use of snowmobiles and all other motorized recreational vehicles on the Club property. Rules can be ignored, but disregarding the bylaws carries weight. This is the wisest way to get my point across. I never want to see animals flying in terror or running for cover from a screaming, polluting snowmobile.

July 4, 1998 • Last night I dream about organizing a huge spiritual event, but then losing focus and failing. The Dalai Lama tells me that something is wrong with my hearing. What am I not hearing?

July 20, 1998 • The day is exquisite with Canadian breezes blowing from the northwest. Everything gleams. From my kayak, I watch the eagle ride the air currents over the big lake. An otter, clenching a cattail in its teeth, swims past. This afternoon, I watch the bluebirds feed their young.

I love having a horse in my life again. My childhood returns though Nell. I'm so taken by her willingness. Willingness is everything.

September 6, 1998 • Today at the Club's annual meeting, the bylaws proposal that I submitted to the Executive Committee passes—but why the membership doesn't oust the president is beyond me. This whole issue isn't just about the environment. It's also about integrity.

No man was ever wise by chance.

Seneca

September 10, 1998 • Ciao has a lot of pain while getting up this morning. It rains on the way to the vet. I'm emotionally low when I pick her up at noon along with a referral to Michigan State University. I call the MSU Veterinary School and get an appointment for Monday the 21st.

September 18, 1998 • Here, in this little cabin in the woods, my clients find the natural balance within themselves that nature demonstrates. May I one day find in myself the deep rootedness of a tree that can shelter others during the storms of their lives.

September 21, 1998 • I arrive with Ciao at MSU on time. My poor dog gets poked, prodded, x-rayed, and blood sampled. Her diagnosis is discospondylosis. We drive the four hours back to the cabin and go for a short walk in the dark. Pain or no pain, Labs live to follow their nose. I take a lesson from her. Now, what did I do with my nose? It's here somewhere.…

September 23, 1998 • More and more clients come to the cabin for Higher GroundWork (as I call Higher Self sessions now.) I don't have much time left before the return to Santa Fe. The maples at the edge of the lakes are exchanging their summer green for autumn red and gold. The wildlife is quieting down. And then, there's my annual melancholy in departing from the woods and water.

A better sense of who I am is taking root inside me. I also feel that my work may be calling for some kind of a change. There might be a need for a new form in my work to emerge. As above, so below. As within, so without. Higher GroundWork will show me where to go and how to get there.

> I was gaining strength as I gained altitude.
>
> Jamling Tenzing Norgay, "Touching My Father's Soul:
> A Sherpa's Journey to the Top of Everest"

Sherpa Norbu's Parable

As Shaypa treks behind me, she focuses on the mark that my boots make in the trail. Even though I am of slight build, my footprints hold so firmly to the earth that the wind does not easily blow them away.

"My mother made these boots and gave them to me for my eighteenth birthday," I tell her, following her gaze to my feet. "That was the day that I began my apprenticeship on the mountain with my father."

Shaypa inspects my boots more closely. The soles are made of yak skin, with thick felt uppers securely sewn to the tops of each boot. Crescent moons are stitched to fully encircle the tops. Soft rawhide strings draw the lunar symbols around the calves of my legs.

Even though they have accumulated a thick layer of dust, Shaypa wonders how one pair of boots could hold up so well for so many steps on mountain paths. These boots are still certain and firm to my feet. As we walk, Shaypa regards my posture: despite my long apprenticeship as a porter, carrying heavy loads for climbers, my back is still as straight and strong as it can be.

Shaypa thinks about how she herself has become stronger since beginning her ascent from base camp seven years ago, about how she can walk in a way that allows her to go farther without having to go faster. She has learned the mountain's unforgiving response to short cuts that she has sometimes tried to make, and how it rewards her efforts to walk correctly and consciously. My patient and practical guidance has also taught her how to travel upon rocky ground with solid and certain steps. But then, Shaypa is willing to walk rugged terrain. She is willing to take on the experiences that the mountain offers and reap the wisdom that they confer.

Seeing her still regarding my boots, I instruct her to look down through her own boots, right through the soles of her feet into the earth. As Shaypa does so, she suddenly transforms into a tree. Her head becomes the crown and her backbone develops a thick taproot. Her body becomes the strong trunk, anchored solidly into the rock. Her outstretched arms grow branches that extend outward. Shaypa feels like she can reach out in all directions at once—outward, upward and, most importantly, downward. And downward is where her curiosity leads her.

Shaypa merges with her great taproot and disappears into the earth. As she descends through what seems to be infinite layers of soil and rock, she revisits each step she has taken in her life. Sometimes her steps have been too short, and sometimes they have been too long, making her trek more difficult than it needed to be. None of her steps however, was ever made in vain.

Eventually, she arrives at an underground river that is deeper than deep has ever been known to be. As she dips her taproot into the river, it takes up the golden sap flowing by. Shaypa has been led by her curiosity to the very source of her strength!

Then, returning to the rock ledge and her human body, Shaypa can no longer deny what she has become. And now she also knows why my boots never wear out and how I remain as straight and strong as ever.

SLEEPING TREES

Pale the moonlight
wraps
the sleeping trees,
that breathe
soft midnight airs
through lungs of leaves.

The dark earth holds
embedded
in deep clasp,
their questing roots,
nurtured on knowing, ancient breast,
these suckling children
of her being.

Mysterious
the shadows lie between,
tender shades of darkness
covering in whispered hush,
the nestling's rest.
Long the century
in which they know
their growing
secret, still
beneath the moon.

CHERRY EARLE, NEW ZEALAND

CRISIS OF BALANCE & BELIEFS

Equilibrium Established and Optimism Reborn

THE TERRITORY

Balance: A state in which various elements form a satisfying and harmonious whole and nothing is out of proportion or unduly emphasized at the expense of the rest

Belief: An opinion, especially a firm and considered one

YOUR APPROXIMATE AGE

North Travel Group	1936-1946	48
South Travel Group	1947-1957	48
East Travel Group	1958-1968	48
West Travel Group	1969-1979	48

TIME IN TRANSIT

Begins a twelve-year cycle

WHAT TO PACK OR ACQUIRE ALONG THE WAY

Physical:	Moderation
Mental:	Non-attachment
Emotional:	Evenness
Spiritual:	Curiosity

WHAT TO LEAVE BEHIND

Excess of anything

THE WEATHER FORECAST

Variable

THE MANTRA

I believe that I can change my mind.

Travel Itinerary

A renewal of beliefs and optimism recurs every twelve years during your life. The Crisis of Balance and Beliefs occurs at age forty-eight and marks your fourth twelve-year cycle. Like the others, it directs you to further expansion and experiences by way of a more positive outlook.

At this time, life also affords you the opportunity to trade in outmoded beliefs for new ones. From approximately age forty-seven through forty-nine, you may have experiences—some subtle and some not so subtle—that challenge you to identify those beliefs that are past their "sell-by" date.

The Crisis of Balance and Belief is, in many ways, akin to the Death Zone on a mountain (that area through which all climbers must ascend in order to reach the summit and return safely to base camp.) It is in the Death Zone that the lives of most climbers are lost due to lapses in judgment, disregard for mortal limits, carelessness, personal hubris, or circumstances beyond their control. Even if you are experiencing circumstances beyond your control, life still invites you to consider renewing your attitudes and beliefs to navigate this crisis in the best possible way. Experienced trekkers maintain the middle path and keep their backpack balanced to improve their chances of reaching the summit safely.

Here's a question for reflection:

> *What habits, attitudes, or beliefs are you carrying that might be affecting your ability to make good judgments, maintain a healthy respect for your limits, and keep any tendencies toward ego inflation in check?*

If your life is showing signs of instability at this time, it might be time to review and renew your beliefs and regain your balance. Check in with your Higher Self; it can often see what you might not with its ability to reveal the beliefs, habits, or tendencies that are operating to your detriment. It can (and will) also show you that your heart space is the place to rekindle your faith in yourself and in the forces that are at work on your behalf.

Ultimately, the experiences that you have during the Crisis of Balance and Beliefs offer you the opportunity to expand your horizons with renewed understanding and optimism, the balance to better carry your higher life purpose on to the Crisis of Contribution and the enthusiasm to accomplish it!

ESSENTIAL TRAVEL TIPS

- Take inventory of outworn beliefs or unbalanced habits as events and circumstances challenge them. Allow them to be replaced by those relevant to your personal growth for the next twelve years.

- Be inspired to become a better someone who aspires toward a better future.

- Expand and grow through ethics, inclusiveness, and an expansive worldview.

- Be the buoyant, broad mind that lifts the world above cynicism and negativity.

- Maintain a heartfelt acceptance of diversity and keep your attention focused toward universality.

The Ultimate Travel Tip:

Maintain a positive attitude and find the higher meaning in everything that happens.

The attachment to views is the greatest impediment to the spiritual path.
Thich Nhat Hanh

SIGHTS AND SOUNDS

This is a short list of the kinds of things that you will find along the way through the Crisis of Balance and Beliefs. You can recognize them as personal traits in yourself or as symbolic messages in your dreams. You are free to choose which of these can be of real and lasting help for the rest of your journey.

Abundance	Credentials	Happiness	Prestige
Achievements	Decency	Harmony	Pride
Acquisitions	Education (higher)	Honor	Principles
Affluence	Enthusiasm	Hope	Prosperity
Auspiciousness	Esteem	Hospitality	Protection
Awards	Ethics	Humor	Recklessness
Balance	Exaggeration	Hubris	Restoration
Beliefs	Excellence	Inheritance	Reverence
Benefits	Excess	Inflation	Rewards
Benevolence	Expansion	Judgment	Self-esteem
Betterment	Expansiveness	Justice	Self-indulgence
Blessings	Expenditures	Laziness	Spendthrifts
Bonuses	Fairness	Loyalty	Success
Carelessness	Faith	Merit	Surplus
Celebrations	Friendliness	Morality	Tact
Cheerfulness	Fortune	Obesity	Travel (foreign)
Compensation	Generosity	Optimists	Virtue
Complacency	Goodness	Over-confidence	Vows
Confidence	Goodwill	Passports	Wealth
Counselor	Gratitude	Philanthropy	Worship
(religious or	Greed	Philosophy	
spiritual)	Growth	Praise	

TRAVELING COMPANIONS

MOTHER TERESA, INDIA

When she was forty-six years of age, Mother Teresa's spiritual director, Cardinal Lawrence Trevor Picachy, advised her to write of her dark and painful inner life in order to better cope with her experience. At the age of forty-eight, Mother Teresa shared these, her personal writings, with Father Picachy:

" 'In the darkness…

Lord, my God, who am I that you should forsake me? The child of your love—and now become as the most hated one—the one You have thrown away as unwanted—unloved. I call, I cling, I want—and there is no One to answer—No One on whom I can cling—no, No One.—Alone. The darkness is so dark—and I am alone.—Unwanted, forsaken.—The loneliness of the heart that wants love is unbearable.—Where is my faith?—Even deep down, right in, there is nothing but emptiness & darkness.—My God—how painful is this unknown pain. It pains without ceasing.—I have no faith.—I dare not utter the words and thoughts that crowd in my heart—and make me suffer untold agony. So many unanswered questions live within me—I am afraid to uncover them—because of the blasphemy—If there be God,—please forgive me.—Trust that all will end in heaven with Jesus.—When I try to raise my thoughts to Heaven—there is such convicting emptiness that those very thoughts return like sharp knives & hurt my very soul.—Love—the word—it brings nothing.—I am told that God loves me—and the reality of darkness & cold & emptiness is so great that nothing touches my soul. Before the work started—there was so much union—love—faith—trust—prayer—sacrifice.—Did I make the mistake in surrendering blindly to the call of the Sacred Heart? The work is not a doubt—because I am convinced that it is His not mine.—I don't feel— not even a single thought or temptation enters my heart to claim anything in the work.

The whole time smiling—Sisters & people pass such remarks.—They think my faith, trust and love are filling my very being & that intimacy with God and union to His will must be absorbing my heart.—Could they but know—and how my cheerfulness is the cloak by which I cover the emptiness and misery.

In spite of all—this darkness & emptiness is not as painful as the longing for God.—The contradiction I fear will unbalance me.—What are you doing My God to one so small? When you asked to imprint Your Passion on my heart—is this the answer?

If this brings You glory, if You get one drop of joy from this—if souls are brought to You—if my suffering satiates Your Thirst—here I am Lord, with joy I accept all to the end of life—& I will smile at Your Hidden Face—always."

Mother Teresa's fear that this interior suffering would unbalance her was not realized.

…After her death, a longtime associate observed, "I think balance was one of Mother Teresa's great attributes.…"

Her closeness to God, which she herself could not perceive, was at the root of the stable and serene disposition that others admired in her. The vigor, joy and enthusiasm with which she carried out her responsibilities powerfully influenced those who came in contact with her, especially her sisters and the poor she served.

From *Mother Teresa: Come Be My Light: The Private Writings of the "Saint of Calcutta,"* edited and with commentary by Brian Kolodiejchuk, M.C.

GAIL, UNITED STATES

With each passing year, Gail, a Montessori School teacher, poured more and more of her heart and soul into her work. She became so identified with the founding philosophy of the program that her enthusiasm spilled over into zealousness. As a self-appointed Joan of Arc, Gail could easily imagine throwing herself in front of moving traffic for the sake of her students.

One day she realized that it was ridiculous of her to think that only she could meet the needs of her students. As she thought about the absurdity of this belief, she began to laugh, relieved to be finally stepping out of such impossible shoes to fill. Years later, when she retired, Gail became a Laughter Yoga leader.

LISA, UNITED STATES

Lisa worked as an engineer for an automobile manufacturer. As the only female in her department, she was so dedicated to her job that her friends would tell her that she was married to it. Scarce acknowledgement and praise by her manager drove her to work longer and longer hours.

When she was traveling on business, Lisa slipped in the hotel bathroom, dislocating three vertebrae and puncturing her inner ear. Her injuries left her with permanent vertigo and loss of balance on the left side of her body that required her to walk with a cane; but even using a cane, she could no longer walk without the fear of falling. To make matters worse, her company sought to terminate her employment because she was no longer a "productive powerhouse."

Lying flat on her back in a long recuperation, Lisa was finally able to "hear" what her extreme career ambitions had blocked out for so many years. By healing her relationship with her mother, Lisa would be able to learn how to forgive, becoming softer and more tolerant. Also, she finally had to admit that her rock solid belief that her company would automatically reward her "extra mile" efforts was simply not true. She realized that what she really wanted was to live a spiritual life. Quitting her job, Lisa moved across the country to a community in which she could maintain a better balance between her inner and outer life.

BARACK OBAMA, UNITED STATES

On November 4, 2008, Barack Obama was elected President of the United States. His message was one of hope, optimism, and change for a country seriously out of balance brought on by excess.

McKenzie's Journal

December 15, 1998 • My realtor, Shelly, calls from Leelanau County to tell me that a 200-acre cherry farm has come up for sale. After six years of inner and outer journeys, I use my heart as a compass to relocate from the New Mexico desert to the Lake Michigan shoreline.

January–March 1999 • Three months of arduous negotiations with the owner of the farm come to a successful agreement. Leelanau County, I am coming home.

I think about the Wilderness Gate property that I tried to purchase in Santa Fe, and how devastated I was at my failed dream. What I couldn't see then was that it was fantasy, not fact. Orchards, beaches, woods, and a barn full of horses are the more accurate reflection of who I am. I get the chills thinking back to how certain I was that Wilderness Gate was it.

April–September 1999 • At the farm, the house is being built on an old oat field surrounded on three sides by cherry orchards, Nell is moved up to a friend's place in Traverse City until the barn is built, and I am driving two hours back and forth from the cabin twice a week to check on construction. I'm creating my place. My only worry is whether Ciao will be able to make it across the bridge to this new life with me. It's becoming more and more painful for her to get in and out of the Jeep, so I time my arrival at the farm to coincide with the worker's lunch time. You can't keep a good Lab from the food.

October 12, 1999 • Here at the cabin the oaks and maples sway back and forth as the wind roars through their canopies. I lie in bed and listen. At 4 A.M., Ciao struggles to get up. Outside in the dark, I hold her up so she can urinate. Back inside, we sit together on the kitchen floor with her food bowl between us. I light a fire and stare helplessly at her as she painfully lowers her body onto the floor in front of the fireplace.

I lie next to her and try to listen past my own desires to hers. A bell is ringing; as my sweet girl-dog fades, so does our history. I don't want to let her go, but I don't want her to have to stay just so I can defer the loss of her. She has been my warmth on the bitter cold thresholds of Bill and Diane's deaths. Now we sit together on hers.

As the day goes by, every moment begs for more moments. At 3:00 P.M., she takes labored steps to lie down on her favorite spot in front of the fireplace, but then cannot get up again. Her eyes plead with me. Dear God, is this it? Is she really telling me to let her go?

I call Rex and ask him to come. We lay skin to fur on the floor and wait. Outside, the wind pulls the leaves from their trees and I surrender to what nature is saying. I clutch the precious last few moments of life lingering between me and my dog—faces close, breaths shared, and deep vulnerability possessing us. The fragile threads in my heart that she repaired in my loss of Bill and Diane begin to pull apart. She is departing on the autumn winds without me.

Rex arrives at 4:15. He sits on the floor with us for a few minutes while I stroke her head. And then, she drifts away on the sound of my tear-choked voice telling her how much I love her.

I wrap her in her blanket and carry her across the river while the water rushes relentlessly around my legs, threatening to pull me in. The wind breathes deeply through the branches of the Three Sisters as I place her gently at the base of their trunks—solid sentries that have stood strong over us for twelve-and-a-half years.

October 13, 1999 • Today is cold, with wind and rain. I huddle under the Three Sisters and weep.

Another sleepless night without my sweet dog's dreaming sounds. I cry like I cried with every other loss in my life. None is different to me from another. Loss is loss, because love is love.

October 21, 1999 • Days and tears go by. I don't want to include life into the gulf of grief that I'm in. But then Jill calls from Santa Fe to tell me she's been diagnosed with uterine cancer. This jolts me out of my inertia and shoves me back into life. I'm grateful to be shoved. Life does not wait. I take my still-heavy heart and get going again.

October 23, 1999 • Because of increased demands for Higher Self work from clients here in Michigan, I decide to stay on longer at the cabin. The privilege of being witness to the discovery and embrace of one's spiritual identity surpasses everything else in my life.

I go to the Point to sit with Ciao under the Three Sisters. The river catches leaves as they depart from the trees; life ceaselessly reclaims its infinite forms—and dispassionately informs me that she doesn't belong to me anymore.

October 26, 1999 • Chakrapani Ullal, a jyotishi from a long line of Indian astrologers, meets with me on the phone. From my birth data, he has calculated my Vedic astrological birth chart, the map of my life. For an hour, he reads my positive and negative tendencies. He notes that on March 6, 1993, a seven-and-a-half year cycle in my life called the sade sati began: this is a time of obstacles, hardships, and hard work in order to build strength. My jaw drops. I tell him that my husband took his life on that day. He wasn't surprised. It was just the first of the many initiations to come. He tells me that this period will end (thank God) on July 6, 2000. I cannot wait for that day.

I ask him if he can determine my life purpose from the chart. He tells me that my dharma is that of counselor, guide, and teacher of holistic health and healing. He tells me that I am to be like "the banyan tree" for people, offering shade and respite from the burning rays of the sun. So that's why trees are so important to me—I am to become one.

On my drive up to the farm this afternoon to check on the house construction, I think about what Chakrapani told me. I love my work, but to have it confirmed as my life purpose by an objective, knowledgeable, and esteemed teacher brings a wave of humility that sweeps away self-importance.

November 27–30, 1999 • Fly to Santa Fe and pack the boxes of my now past life and tell them to have a good ride on the moving truck up to Michigan. There's a party at Bruce's. I'm exhausted, but I go anyway. Fly back to Michigan.

December 6, 1999 • The scant snow cover here at the farm makes it easy to get boxes off the truck and into the house. As I unpack each, I realize that I should have gotten rid of a lot more stuff before leaving Santa Fe. Oh, well. On a positive note, forty-three acres of frozen cherry trees will be forty-three acres of cherry blossoms in the spring.

December 23, 1999 • I spend my forty-seventh birthday at the cabin. I snowshoe to the Three Sisters at the river and sit in white silence.

December 24, 1999 • I look in the mirror and notice that I've really aged this last year. My skin is ashen. Is this how you're supposed to look at forty-seven?

December 31, 2000 • New Year's Eve party at the farm for Michigan friends. We're ignoring Y2K predictions of doom and gloom.

January 13, 2000 • While Karen and I are riding today, I ask her to have her husband, Tim, look at a lump that I found in my left breast yesterday. I lie on the sofa in their living room as he tries to aspirate fluid from the lump with a syringe. Nothing comes out. He tells me that it's probably just hormonal changes, but that I should get a mammogram. I've now had seven mammograms since age thirty-five: one more won't kill me.

February 3, 2000 • Mammogram doesn't "see" the lump. How is that possible? They do an ultrasound and it shows up. What the hell? Biopsy scheduled for tomorrow.

February 7, 2000 • The surgeon is young. Before doing the biopsy he arrogantly announces that he knows that it's better than a fifty-fifty chance that the lump is malignant. I'm sitting half-naked on the table as he delivers the unsolicited opinion. What a punch of insensitivity. Then he does a biopsy. On my way out, my last words to him are: "Whether it is or isn't, you're fired."

February 9, 2000 • I'm diagnosed with breast cancer today. My bed is the only place I want to be.

February 10, 2000 • Cancer. This can't be happening. I want any way out of this. Just as I'm making a new life here in Michigan, I'm going to die?

I drive to the cabin in surreal slow motion. I escape into bed at 9 P.M. only to awaken at 11 P.M., drenched in a cold sweat and paralyzed with fright from a nightmare. In it, I am sitting in my chair in the cabin, looking out over the lake below. Two snowmobiles race at a death-defying speed from one end of the lake to the other. I notice five people, obviously trespassers, standing at the edge of the lake. I feel violated but I go down to confront them and tell them to leave immediately. As they turn toward me, I recoil: their faces are grotesquely deformed. One of them has no nose. I scream at them to leave but they refuse. Impotence, fear, and frustration freeze me in my tracks, leaving me unable to defend myself.

I wake up and light a candle next to the bed, hoping the flame will drive out the intense fear that is clamping every cell of my body shut. I remember how Sai Baba had healed Gay Luce's eyesight when she was at his ashram in India many years ago. I call inwardly to him to please help me … and help me NOW. A small voice whispers to me that this is happening to save my life. This makes no sense to me.

I wake up this morning to the unmistakable scent of jasmine drifting under my nose. From my studies at Nine Gates Mystery School, I remember that jasmine is associated with the presence of Sai Baba in the same way that vibhuti, or sacred ash, is also associated with him. Has Sai Baba actually come to me? I clutch for more of the fragrance as it fades. My desperation is beyond words.

> This is how humans are: we question all our beliefs except for the ones we really believe, and those we never think to question.
>
> Orson Scott Card

I drink coffee in my chair overlooking the lake, the same chair from which I had seen the snowmobiles and trespassers in my nightmare. I urgently need to understand what it means. I think hard about the snowmobiles and how they tore across the lake at such an outrageous speed. I hate snowmobiles. I recall the battle that I had with the president of the club two years ago. What were these snowmobiles doing in my dream now?

Oh, no. OH NO—the insane pace that I've sustained in this past year! Negotiating for and purchasing the farm, designing and building the house, moving Nell up north, attending to clients, going through Ciao's death, moving from one state to another, and hitting and killing two deer. The snowmobile that I detest for its speed, noise, and pollution is, in fact, the one I'm using to drive my life at breakneck speed. I have crossed the centerline and caused a wreck—and I'm the wreck! The deformed trespassers in my dream are obviously the trespassing malignancy in my left breast. Dear God.

February 10, 2000 • I call the surgeon who operated on Diane when she was diagnosed with breast cancer. Surgery is set for February 15th.

I call my friend Robert, the man with whom I'd had a wonderful relationship for two years. Despite the fact that we are no longer together, his kind response is immediate. If anyone can lend me strength he can. I call my friend Kathryn and tell her the news. She also comes forward without hesitation. Cancer is something that no one wants to be touched by, much less touch. Yet here they are, both Scorpios, the ones who can stand with me in this dark and scary place. I have to work unbelievably hard to prevent my mind from wandering into terrible future scenarios.

Robert arrives at the cabin to be with me, to listen as I speak out loud what I need to say. The question of whether I will live or die sits between us. I do not know. He does not know. Bill has died, Diane has died, and Ciao has died. Will I now die?

February 12, 2000 • Many people diagnosed with a life-threatening illness such as cancer ask the question, "Why me?" Why now?" I'm the one now asking those questions. The only place to get the true answers is my Higher Self. I know, as a facilitator of this work, that the source of my healing lies in the roots of my illness. I'm going to find those roots, if it's the last thing I do on this earth. I find this quote in one my books by Carl Jung: "Healing proceeds from the depths to the heights." I'm going to proceed.

It's important for me to do a session before the surgery so that I can take the shift in consciousness into the operating room. Kathryn agrees to facilitate my session—we set up a healing space at the cabin. When she is ready with her paper and a pen to scribe, I lie back under flannel sheets on the massage table and close my eyes to the outer world. The inner landscape appears immediately, almost urgently:

> I'm standing on a country lane lined with ancient stone
> walls. Despite the fact that it's a cool, misty day, my feet
> are hot as if I am standing in fire. I look out on fields
> to see an entire landscape of rotting potatoes. There is a
> sense of hopelessness in me that descends from my heart
> to my stomach. I am hungry, hungrier that I have ever
> been, but I don't even bother climbing the wall to look

for anything that may still be edible. I'm stuck in this place of resignation.

A few scrawny dogs wander by, scavenging for food. But one dog walks straight to me and knocks me in the back of my knees with its nose. I look down at him and he meets my gaze directly. As I reach for him, he backs away. He doesn't need me to pick him up. Instead, he starts off in the opposite direction. I turn around and follow him. He puts his nose to the ground to track something unseen, yet definitely present. His nose is perfectly attuned to whatever is drawing him forward. Even though I can't see it, he very much "sees" it with his nose. He follows it over the stone wall into one of the fields. I stay with him as he takes me directly into a field of rotting potatoes. The deep muck doesn't bother the dog, but it really bothers me. As I walk through it, the potatoes break up into stinking clods of waste under my feet. The soles of my feet seem destined to meet and become intimate with these rotting potatoes.

Before my eyes, the clods transform into the corpses of my ancestors. I'm walking right on top of them. I'm walking on all of their sadness, hopelessness, hunger, and confusion. I cannot separate myself from it! I sink up to my knees in the thick, black mess and fear that I will get sucked down into this desolate, rotting graveyard. The time here seems endless. When will I ever be released from this slog across old graves and sad stories? I struggle against the pull of the soil and a cold sweat wraps me tightly, threatening to doom me to this hell forever.

The dog has almost disappeared from sight and I desperately try to pull myself out of the muck to catch up with him. But the field never seems to end. How much farther do I have to go?

I realize that these fields are my own flesh and bones. There is no separation between my ancestors and me. Their stories are my story. I am the lineage bearer of the ways of my ancestors. The mud is so deep and so dark. It covers me from head to toe. I'm a mess. My clothes are ripped, wet, and filthy. I am so exhausted I can hardly walk. I feel lost and at the end of life.

The dog is far out in front of me and still I'm hopelessly bogged in the sucking mud. "God help me, I might lose the dog," I gasp to myself. "Stop, wait," I cry weakly to him.

Instantly, the dog is at my side. The invisible track that he has been following leads us up and over the stone wall and onto the road again. We're suddenly out of the field. I'm tired. I'm exhausted. I have to sit down. I'm so relieved. Something has pulled me to safety. I am back on stable ground without knowing how I got there. I look down at my feet. My shoes are gone. The godforsaken mud has claimed them.

On the other side of the road is a creek. The dog plunges in and I follow. The rushing water is colder than I have ever known cold to be. This mud is difficult to wash off my skin. I keep working at it, but I can never completely clean it out of my pores. It's the best I can do for now. I'm different when I emerge from the creek. I am clean for the most part, but some of the soil remains to remind me of the substance of my lineage.

The dog begins to circle around my legs, first to the left

and then to the right, joining me to him with an invisible thread. He starts down the road again. As I follow, I realize that I have to take smaller steps or I will lose my balance. I'm trying to see the wisdom in this new way of walking. I have to be mindful of my steps or I will fall.

Dust kicks up from my footsteps. Suddenly a glint of light reflects off something in the road. I look down to see a coin, partially obscured by the dust. I bend over and pick it up. I study it closely for a minute and note that it is gold on one side and silver on the other. It's newly minted, but blank. It is like a hybrid, having both gold and silver within one coin. I get a strong sense that this coin is very much itself: it knows itself fully and completely as a coin. It has no mark, no inscription, nothing that says what it is worth. The significance of this coin is that it does not have signification on it. Therefore, it can be of any value to anyone who picks it up. Far from being useless, it can be quite useful. The coin's actual value is limitless and infinite. Its only responsibility is to be a coin lying silently in the road to be either walked past or picked up. The energy of the coin is exactly neutral, but its value is infinite. This seems both important and paradoxical. As I pick up the coin and put it in my left breast pocket, I become the coin...

It is dark in this pocket; I am alone in here. I am feeling the heart of this woman beating underneath Me as I lay in her pocket. I become synchronized with her heart's rhythm. As her heart opens, My essence shines through it. An exchange is taking place between my infinite value and her heart. I'm just a simple coin found on a dusty road in the land of her ancestors. She's the one who picked Me up. She's the one who put me next to her heart, taking me to heart. She recognizes my infinite value amidst the immeasurable poverty of her ancestors. She didn't pick Me up by mistake. She picked Me up because she saw that I was there. What a simple but powerful act!

She chose to see goodness in Me, rather than sadness and despair, this woman. She was willing to bend over and pick Me up, to put Me into her pocket. She did not throw Me back onto the road. She trusted a blank coin with seemingly no value and saw it as something of infinite value. Underneath the hopelessness of her ancestors she found hope in Me—a simple, faceless coin. She saw potential in Me, saw abundance in Me, saw her Self in Me. That is how she recognized Me in the first place, or she never would have seen Me. This one sees Me in herself in the land of her ancestors. And now I am here in her pocket—intimate with her beating heart.

Some people recognize that she's got something in her pocket and she is always glad to take it out and show it to them. What they see is a blank coin and, of course, the rest is up to them—to see into Me and to see what I am for them. It's about inheritance. And she now knows that I, not her ancestors, am her true inheritance. That's what she chose to see.

But she would never have found Me without being willing to slog across the graves and dark days of her ancestors. Her steps across that field were difficult and painful, but that is how she found Me. Her willingness to shorten her steps was enough to see Me, so she could claim Me as her real and rightful inheritance.

I come out of my deep state brushing away something that I feel on my face. I look at my hands. Ash. Ash? I pick up my head to make out a fine layer of ash also on the blanket. I look back at Kathryn on the sofa behind me, and see ash on her. It's all over the room. I drop my head back on the table in disbelief. It's vibhuti—the sacred ash of Sai Baba.

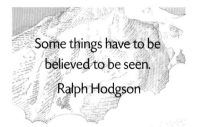

Some things have to be believed to be seen.

Ralph Hodgson

To see everything as metaphor helps me to understand what is happening. The presence of vibhuti all over the room and its association with the presence of Sai Baba can be looked at in this way: Sai Baba is an avatar, a divine being, one who can perform miracles because his mind is free of all obstructions. Sai Baba is said to be a living manifestation of Christ-consciousness. Jesus the Christ once said, "The kingdom is within." To me, this means that only with a mind free of obstructions—judgment, attachment, and aversion—can I access the "kingdom."

Is it possible that in clearing away so much of my flawed consciousness (the seeds of my self-undoing) that I was able to touch the Source? Does my experience in the session and the manifestation of the vibhuti indicate that? Cancer, the unanticipated, paradoxical healer, offered me this experience. I was willing to go as deep with it as it needed to take me. I could never dream in a million years that I would find what I found in myself—the silver and gold coin of the perfect balance of masculine and feminine energy.

To release flawed, indoctrinated beliefs of ancestry and culture is to restore balance to both…one person at a time.

February 15, 2000 • Robert drives me the three hours to the hospital in Grand Rapids. On the way, an eagle crosses overhead! I take it into myself and hold it close as a good omen. Check in for outpatient surgery in the middle of the afternoon. Surgery scheduled for 4 P.M. I hold the written transcript of my last session, reading it with single-minded focus while I

"There is no use trying," said Alice. "I cannot believe in impossible things."

"I dare say you haven't had much practice," said the Queen. "When I was your age, I always did it for half an hour a day. Why, sometimes I've believed in as many as six impossible things before breakfast."

from "Alice in Wonderland," by Lewis Carroll

wait for Dr. DeKryger to arrive. Nothing else in the room exists as I concentrate on the coin as the healing source within my consciousness. I know that I have to "pick up" or choose the coin in order to heal the imbalances at the root of my illness.

Two orderlies wheel me into the operating room and shift me over to the table. I think how interesting it is that both spiritual and medical healing takes place on tables. The nurses position my left arm out straight out from my side to expose the surgery site. They stretch my right arm out for IVs in the same way. Here I lie, like one upon the cross. A perfect crucifixion—regarded by some in my field as a "crossing out" of old consciousness for a rebirth of new consciousness. I now believe that. I look up at Dr. DeKryger as he takes my left hand to hold it gently in his. His entire being becomes compassion itself. Oh, my God.

I wake up to the nurse working with the IV in my hand. Robert and Kathryn stand on each side of the bed, staring down at me. They wait for me to say something, but I'm waiting for them to say something. And all I want to know, of course, is what Dr. DeKryger told them about how the surgery went. Robert tells me that it came out cleanly and easily, but that it was sizable. The pathology report will be back on Friday.

At 9 P.M. I break out of the hospital and to the cabin we three go. I feel like a truck has hit me. Just like when I was seven years old, driving across the alley on my cousin's brand new bike, right smack into a truck. Broken pelvis (the center of the body's balance.) No surprise that a bicycle also symbol-izes balance. Let's see, that's exactly forty years ago and the tendency is still alive and well and has come home to roost. When *will* I learn? How about right now?

February 18, 2000 • Robert goes home and Kathryn comes to stay with me here at the cabin. She keeps a fire burning in the fireplace all day. We talk, read Rumi, eat, and sleep. The drain tube is a pain in the butt. Wait-ing for the phone call is excruciating. Finally, at 4 P.M., Dr. DeKryger calls with the pathology results: he removed sixteen lymph nodes, and all were clean. I breathe a wide-eyed sigh of relief.

March 28, 2000 • Walking out of the hospital with my pathology slides, I pass a bank of newspaper machines in the lobby. The Detroit Free Press headline, "To Forgive, Divine" sits directly above the Chicago Tribune with its headline, "Complete Remission." I stop. I stare. The perfect juxtaposition of these captions

I can believe in anything as long as it's incredible.
Oscar Wilde

gives me the one vital and universal truth I need to get right now. And I get it loud and clear.

March 29, 2000 • Back at the cabin, I embark on a radical forgiveness process extending to everyone I can possibly think of, including myself. How intimate are forgiveness and freedom; forgiveness is essential if I am to be truly free. Now I know why my Inner Child gave me "freedom" as a gift in my first session at the Light Institute almost ten years ago. It knew what I needed the most, and only now I discover that forgiveness is what I need to do to acquire it.

March – May, 2000 • In my search for an oncologist, I meet two grue-some characters in medical doctor masks. One is a woman who is a physical and emotional mess and vastly more unhealed than I; the other is a fatalist. They insist that chemotherapy is absolutely necessary, despite the fact that all sixteen lymph nodes are clean. They maintain that it's necessary just in case one little cell has escaped into my body. For now, chemo is out of the question. I feel like I'm being bulldozed by pharmaceutical propaganda spreading fear and paranoia. I finally find a doctor who is positive and who offers me the reins of my own life. I start seven weeks of radiation on Monday. I just can't see chemo right now.

I receive a range of holistic therapies. The most healing aspect of each process is the practitioner—skilled, compassionate, respectful, and unafraid of my process. I'm not looking for a cure. I either will or won't be cured. Cures are secondary to healing. My task right now is to dissolve the theme that drives the pattern leading to this "dis-ease." If I heal the theme, then I can restore my body's equilibrium.

May 5, 2000 • I'm getting ready to go to La Jolla, California, to the Deepak Chopra Center for my next healing experience. I have not been able to accept doing chemotherapy, so I'm hoping David Simon M.D., Deepak's partner, will tell me that I don't need to do it.

May 8, 2000 • Did not sleep well last night but I am ready to begin an ayurvedic healing process with others also being challenged by cancer. At the start of the week's program everyone is gathered in the lobby, drinking tea, and getting to know each other. After a building tour and introduction by David Simon and some of the other facilitators, I receive an ayurvedic massage and attend a lecture on mind/body principles.

This afternoon, each of us in the class will receive our personal mantras from the Vedic tradition. I receive mine in Deepak's office from Midge, one of the facilitators. The room is neither large nor ostentatious. My mantra is derived from the exact time, date and geographical location of my birth to indicate the precise phase of the moon. Each phase of the moon has a distinct "universal sound," as heard by the ancient rishis (Hindu sages) of India in their meditations. I am advised to keep my mantra private to avoid scattering its sacred energy, in the same way as we hold sacred the details of Higher Self sessions.

May 9, 2000 • Morning meditation. Ayurvedic cooking classes. Ayurvedic therapies. More meditation.

May 10, 2000 • It is the last day of the program. Roger, a facilitator, counsels me that the finest steel comes from the hottest fire. Right now I feel like a heap of old, rusted auto parts. He also tells me that to worry is to pray for the things you don't want. Yeah, worry is one of my favorite things to do and it's got to go—for good.

May 12, 2000 • The final day of our class. We say good-bye to each other. I have to stay until Monday in order to meet with David Simon. I pray that he doesn't tell me that I have to do chemotherapy.

May 13, 2000 • I eat breakfast, meditate, and walk on the beach. Before I go to bed I write a letter to Sai Baba asking for insight. I have two dreams. In the first, I'm on an indoor tennis court. My partner has brought tennis balls (beliefs?) that are old, dirty, ripped, and basically unplayable. Angry that she has brought these, I go to the pro shop and buy new ones.

In the second dream, I am in a hardware store. I have a load of heavy objects (beliefs/habits/tendencies?) that I want to put down. I find a small shelf, but I think to myself, "I've already purchased these! Am I supposed to leave behind what I've already purchased?" I feel badly about leaving these objects behind because I have made an investment in them. But what I am really putting down is the burden of old beliefs, not the investment.

While the dreams are still fresh, I sit in bed and inventory my beliefs. They have become a burden, especially and obviously to my body. What new beliefs do I now want to invest in that will be lighter and more balanced to carry?

May 14, 2000 • My morning walk takes me by the city tennis courts where an older man has just finished playing. I ask him to tell me the secret of his longevity. His reply is, "I'm eighty-four years old. I don't drink much, I don't chase money, I don't chase women, I get plenty of sleep, and I play only two sets of tennis at a time." How's that for walking right up to my own billboard? Think I'll start playing tennis.

May 15, 2000 • I have a dream about acceptance last night. This morning, I have my meeting with David Simon. He gets right to the point after reading my pathology report. In contradiction to all other statistics given me previously, he quotes an 82 percent survival rate for my type of cancer at five years. He encourages me to do the chemotherapy though, saying that I'll sail right through it. Okay, okay. Acceptance. All things can happen from the field of infinite possibilities when an internal shift is made.

May 17, 2000 • I fly home from Deepak's Center a very changed person. Kathryn picks me up at the airport and we arrive at the farm around midnight. The moon is almost full and it illuminates the horses grazing in the pasture. Kathryn encourages me to consider getting a new puppy. It's been seven months since Ciao passed away. Am I ready?

May 18, 2000 • Kathryn and I drive to Benzonia to look at Doberman puppies on our way to the cabin.

I want a female, but a little male yelps at us from the whelping box. Kathryn sets him on the floor and he runs straight for me. "My name is Ollie! My name is Ollie!" sounds off in my head. He glues himself to my ankles. "Your name is Ollie?" A Doberman Pinscher named Ollie?

May 27, 2000 • I notice that Ollie's birthmark is in the exact same place on his chest as my tumor was on mine. This is more than interesting.

May 28, 2000 • I take Ollie to the beach at Good Harbor Bay. This puppy is a goofball! Never knew Dobermans to be as fun and funny as this! Did I luck out, or what?

June 9, 2000 • First chemotherapy treatment. To avoid imprinting it, I do not participate in the medical process. Instead, I plug in my CD player, close my eyes, and listen to Hindu healing chants, taking myself into the higher realms of Mind where disease does not exist.

June 20, 2000 • Now I know how the horses feel every spring—my hair is starting to fall out. I go down to the village and ask Deborah to shave my head. This is not a favorite assignment for a hairdresser. She cringes through the entire process. I console her. My hair is gone in two minutes; I look like a Buddhist monk, and that's probably the way it's supposed to be.

According to the *Illustrated Encyclopaedia of Traditional Symbols*, hair represents the powers of thought. Shaving one's head removes old hair (old thoughts) so that new thoughts can grow. It denotes the ascetic or the dedicated person renouncing physical powers to rightly acknowledge or accept spiritual power. This is exactly what is happening to me now. Recognizing the metaphoric significance of things gives me more understanding of my predicament. I cannot think of a better event than disease from which to mine meaning. If I'm going to be ill, I might as well be enlightened by it.

Over the summer there is vulnerability, weakness, strength, comedy, fortitude, and joy. I am alive! With successive Higher Self sessions, I continue to plow under the worn out soils of old consciousness in order to uncover new and fertile earth. I ride Nell and, with my hair gone, the rushing wind across my head is an insanely good feeling as we canter across fields. I'm being relieved by life of my old identity. On the other side of old is new. And that's where my horse and I are headed. I will be victorious.

> The average pencil is seven inches long with just a half-inch eraser—in case you thought that optimism was dead.
>
> Robert Brault

July 6, 2000 • Today is the last day of my seven-and-a-half-year-long sade sati. That I am stronger now than I was prior to March 6, 1993, is an understatement.

August 21, 2000 • My last chemotherapy treatment. I walk out of the office like I'm one of the visitors, not the patient. I do not look back.

March 14, 2001 • I sit on the dock at the cabin with Ollie and a cup of tea to listen. My mind keeps going back and forth about writing a book versus not writing a book. If I am to write a book, then what will I write? What are the parts and pieces of my journey that will serve others on theirs? What value will this book have? My Higher Self tells me to "look down." I look down at the paper tag on my Yogi tea bag. On it are printed the words: "If you do not value your words you have no value. Your word is your value." Got it.

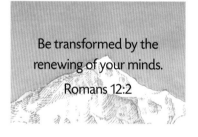

Be transformed by the renewing of your minds.
Romans 12:2

March 24, 2001 • One of my group members from Chopra Institute e-mails today, telling me of a recurrence of her colon cancer. It has spread to her lungs. Somewhere I read that our self-love has to be so strong and true that the suffering of another does not disturb it and detour our thoughts into fear. I think of how many people have run from me when they discovered that I had breast cancer, but in knowing Nance through her life-threatening illness, I have been privileged to witness her powerful spiritual ascension.

April 15, 2001 • Easter Sunday. This morning I dream that Nell has changed. Her solid chestnut color has been transformed into color maps of foreign countries spread out over her body. The hair on the back of my head is shaved into the shape of a four-leaf clover. The clover then changes to a map of a country, and then expands again and again until my entire head is a three-dimensional, color map of the world. The feeling is one of being in perfect union with my soul.

I recall a similar dream I had when I was twelve years old, one that was so vivid and so real it has stayed with me for my entire life. It occurred about a year after my parents bought me my first horse. In the dream, the globe of the world that stood in the corner of my school classroom was suspended in a dark, star filled universe. I was riding my horse all over this globe, all over the world, through every country.

Are these two dreams connected? I think so. At twelve years of age, I entered my first Jupiter Return, the first twelve-year cycle of renewed beliefs. Now, at the age of forty-eight, I am entering my fourth Jupiter Return. The motifs in both dreams are very similar. Horses symbolize freedom and power. The globe of the world symbolizes worldview. The universe in which it was hanging denotes a universal worldview. Riding my horse all over the world gives me a consciousness that is freed by an ever-expanding universal worldview. Attained through foreign travel or travel through the mind, it achieves the same thing.

In my recent dream, the head denotes mind, thoughts, and knowledge. The four-leaf clover symbolizes good fortune. A shaved head denotes the removal of old thoughts (beliefs) that are removed from the mind. The subsequent renewal of beliefs fuels optimism, which inevitably attracts good fortune (some say "luck," but I believe that luck is not random, but the result of accurate beliefs.) Luck is depicted by the four-leaf clover. That the clover transforms into a country and then the entire world tells me that, by renewing my beliefs, I expand my worldview to encompass the entire world. This is universality. The Jupiterian archetype is widely understood as optimism, expansion, and universality. The Jupiter Return, occurring every twelve years, invites every human being to these experiences. This is where I am now. This is what I'm doing and how I move forward. This is why I will succeed. Without the astrological map that describes these cycles and their timing, I would never have been able to put together all of this meaning! My dreams, like my Higher Self sessions, are reflected in the symbols on my astrological birth map and its perfectly synchronized life events. They all say the same thing, just in different ways.

My inner work to expunge the roots of my breast cancer has birthed new beliefs from the ashes of old ones. My habits, spawned by these beliefs— even the unconscious, inherited ones—produced an extreme imbalance between my mind and my body. Cancer did save my life. More accurately, my willingness to follow my Higher Self to the roots of my illness in order to expunge its origins saved my life. How interesting that this fourth Jupiter Return occurred at the exact time of my illness to prompt me to find new beliefs and better balance for the best possible outcome.

April 28, 2001 • I ride Sarah's horse, Cooper, in a jumping clinic this weekend. My soul sings when I'm flying over fences on a horse.

May 1, 2001 • Cabin, kayak, big lake, and some species of birds I haven't seen before. Everything is intensely alive. How does death so vividly illuminate life? Not because death is the end to life, but perhaps because death is the doorway to the source of life. And maybe, when we stand in death's doorway, we see, firsthand, the light of the Source.

June 5, 2001 • I kayak in the afternoon. Ollie runs the path next to the shoreline. At midpoint around the lake, he collides with a newborn fawn hidden under a cedar next to the shore. It leaps away from him, but straight into the water. As I have done so often in the past when Ciao had the same meetings, I paddle furiously to the drenched, kicking, bleating fawn and scoop it into the kayak with me. Impossible to paddle and dodge its tiny, sharp hooves flailing wildly around my chin. I ask the wind to blow me toward shore, and then crawl carefully out of the boat only to sink up to my shins in wonderful black muck. I carry the fawn into the woods and set it down gently under a cedar tree to wait for its mother. This sodden creature, its heart beating wildly, looks the question, "What in the world just happened to me?" I put my face close to hers and reply, "I know that place, little one."

June 21, 2001 • I return from Ann Arbor and get out of the car. Ollie runs up to greet me. I bend over and offer him a female Doberman puppy. Her name is Grace. He gently takes her in his mouth, walks to his bed and commences to wash her. Two Dobermans are double joy. And, as my friend Robert told me when I was diagnosed: never postpone joy. And I add to that: never postpone maintaining the balance of masculine and feminine energies.

July 24, 2001 • Robert and I drive up to Charlevoix to skydive with his son Andy and his crew. This could easily be classified as insane. Nonetheless, in tandem with Andy, I somersault out of the plane from eleven thousand feet into a free fall for six thousand feet before pulling the chute to float in silence over an awesomely beautiful Lake Michigan shoreline. Wow, who am I now? Some would say I'm crazy, but I'd say I'm joy.

Sherpa Norbu's Parable

Shaypa and I are climbing through the Death Zone. The footing is unstable and the weather conditions unpredictable. Shaypa insists that we push on to attain the summit.

I know better. It is time to rest and regroup.

"This is a good place to stop," I advise her, pointing down at the trail.

Shaypa can't even tell it's a grave, except for the mani stone set beside it. Time and the countless treks have so worn the path that climbers walk past without noticing it. This resting place, though unseen by them, is fully witnessed by the mountain.

I whisper to Shaypa, "This is the grave of a climber who died here. Now released from her physical form, her essence is free, but always remains. It is significant that her grave is not set to the side, but is instead placed directly under the footprints of others who are trekking to the summit."

Shaypa stares silently at the stone, not knowing what to say.

I continue, "Through rebirth, she becomes part of this new generation of climbers, and treks over and beyond the bones of her past to make yet another ascent."

"Shaypa," I add, "it is death that offers this climber's essence to future generations. And it is rebirth that provides her with new form and footsteps to become even more of whom she returns to the mountain to be."

This is Shaypa's lesson: in constant death and rebirth, everything continues toward the summit.

Flowers of Tomorrow

I will die in the autumn
when the earth prepares
to sleep,
and the sap pauses
in its aggressive climb
to the outer tips
of the trees.
With the falling leaves
I will go,
my blood and bone will merge
with the regenerating earth,
composting,
to grow the flowers of tomorrow.

Cherry Earle, New Zealand

CRISIS OF CONTRIBUTION
The Gift in the Wound

THE TERRITORY
A voluntary gift

YOUR APPROXIMATE AGE

North Travel Group	(1936-1946)	50
South Travel Group	(1947-1957)	50
East Travel Group	(1958-1968)	50
West Travel Group	(1969-1979)	50

TIME IN TRANSIT
One year

WHAT TO PACK OR ACQUIRE ALONG THE WAY

Physical: Vitality
Mental: Awareness
Emotional: Integrity
Spiritual: Love, Compassion, and Generosity

WHAT TO LEAVE BEHIND
The urge to escape, deny, or disown your wound

THE WEATHER FORECAST
Blizzard conditions or clear skies

THE MANTRA
My song changes the world.

TRAVEL ITINERARY

Robert Kowal discovered Chiron, a planetoid, on November 1, 1977, orbiting on an elliptical path between Saturn and Uranus. Chiron completes one full orbit around the Sun every 50.7 years, thus taking exactly this long to "return" to its point of origination.

In the astrological world, when a heavenly body is discovered, it indicates that humanity, as a collective, is ready to integrate the "symbolic function" of that planet into life on earth. This symbolic function can be considered an archetype—a set of characteristics.

Discovery is intimately linked to a readiness to "see," and therefore integrate what we see "above" (in the heavens) into our lives "below" (on earth.) Through the lens of astrology, we can observe these planetary archetypes in both our personal lives and in society as a whole. In the horoscope, Chiron's symbol, or glyph, is a key; the top half is the letter K, to denote the K in the discoverer's last name, Kowal. The K stands atop an oblong circle, denoting the elliptical shape of Chiron's orbit.

Chiron's archetype is holism—the view that integration of all aspects of our human nature creates wholeness. Since its discovery, the world has indeed seen the rise of countless holistic healing modalities, including integrative medicine—the integrative relationship between mind and body. As a centaur—half-man–half-horse—Chiron symbolizes the state of wholeness that is possible when intellect and instinct (mind and body) co-exist in balance and harmony. Resurgence in vitality and creativity is experienced when this is achieved.

In early Greek mythology, Chiron was the first centaur and eventually became the leader of the race of centaurs. Known for his patience, wisdom and self-mastery, he instructed and mentored Achilles, Aneas, Asclepius, Heracles, Jason, and Peleus. To them and others, he taught the arts of hunting, horsemanship, medicine, holistic healing, music, astronomy, and astrology.

In an abridged version of the story, Chiron was wounded in the leg one day by an errant arrow let fly by Heracles during a skirmish that broke out among the band of centaurs. Unfortunately, the tip of the arrow had been tainted by the poisonous blood of the Hydra, whom Heracles had killed in an earlier battle. Because he was immortal, Chiron could not die, and thus suffered great pain. Thereafter, Chiron was characterized as a "wounded healer."

His experience teaches that we are all subject to life's woundings, no matter how unfair they may seem. However, if we want to remain vital, we can use the pain of our wounds as a catalyst to become more conscious. This is called "the healing journey," since healing is synonymous with evolving our consciousness toward a state of wholeness.

The Chiron wound in particular has both pitfalls, arising from lack of awareness, and potentials, obtained through awareness. By being willing to become aware, you can live creatively through your wound's potentials, rather than fall prey to its pitfalls. Thus, when you lack awareness of your Chiron wound, your Chiron wounding will repeat over and over in order to gain your attention. If, however, you become aware of your Chiron wound, you can discover and offer its many potentials as your contribution.

Throughout your life up to the age of fifty, you will experience six minor and three major Chiron events. These experiences leave a deep mark in you and influence the course of your life. Each Chiron event is part of the Chiron cycle, and together, they define your specific "wounded healer" theme. This theme provides another level of meaning and purpose to your life story. Your life map describes the specific area of your life in which your Chiron wound exists, how it expresses itself, and when each event occurs.

Melanie Reinhart, in her book *Chiron and the Healing Journey: An Astrological and Psychological Perspective*, describes the three major Chiron events leading up to the Crisis of Contribution:

FIRST EVENT

This is the initial event that brings wounding at the hands of parents, teachers, or other authority figures. Although you may not be able to understand or avoid its pain, this is the wounding that points you in the direction of the next event, from which you can discover more about your life.

SECOND EVENT

The years leading up to this event are ideal for resolving any physical, mental, emotional, psychological, and spiritual imbalances. If you have not done this work, a crisis may occur to get you to correct any unresolved issues in your life. If you have done your work, you can expect to detect the first suggestion about the greater meaning of your life.

THIRD EVENT

This event gives you another opportunity to unite your instincts—your body wisdom—with your intellect. If you accomplish this, you can manifest your creative potential in powerful ways. With more understanding and maturity under your belt, you can now also get a better sense of your place in the world.

Then comes the Chiron Return—the Crisis of Contribution—that takes place at the age of fifty for everyone. This is a major turning point that represents the "return" of Chiron in your life. By discovering the theme of your wound and the area of your life in which it exists, you can combine your Chiron potentials with any other of your unique skills and talents and offer them in just the way that the world needs them. And remember, there are countless paths to wholeness. Your path is as valid as any other, so trust your own way.

THE CHIRON RETURN: THE CRISIS OF CONTRIBUTION

Reinhart describes some occurrences that happen at the time of the Chiron Return:

- Old wounds and unresolved issues may arise for acknowledgement and healing.

- Abandoned aspirations are reclaimed and/or re-formed.

- The will to live is tested.

- The realization of time wasted and opportunities lost either precipitates depression or catalyzes action.

- A lack of interest or responsibility for your life is confronted.

- Mortality is faced through illness, disease, or death.

- Anger or resentment for pain caused by earlier wounding that has not yet been acknowledged erupts into illness, depression, or psychological narrowness.

- Wounding others, or being wounded by others, can occur.

- A broader and deeper participation in life is activated.

- The quest for individuation or spirituality is taken up in earnest.

- The question, "What am I going to do with the remainder of my life?" is asked, and answered.

- The meaning of your life comes into clearer focus and flourishes.

- Your talents, skills, and gifts positively influence the lives of others.

ESSENTIAL TRAVEL TIPS

- Be willing to resolve those issues in your life that are still unresolved.
- Lay painful memories to rest.
- Recognize the lessons and gifts in your wounds.
- Enlist your skills, gifts, and talents and offer them to others.
- See everything as a gift.
- Recognize that everything is unified.

Ultimate Travel Tip:

Love and compassion are the ultimate contributions.

True power is wisdom found in remembering your total journey. Wisdom comes from remembering the pathway that you have walked in another person's moccasins. Compassion, caring, teaching, loving and sharing your gifts, talents and abilities are the gateway to power.

from "The Horse," Chapter 35 in "Medicine Cards,"
by Jamie Sams

SIGHTS AND SOUNDS

This is a list of the kinds of things that you may find along the way through the Crisis of Contribution. You can recognize these as personal traits or as symbolic messages in your dreams. You are free to choose which of these can be of real and lasting value for the rest of your life journey.

Anger	Holistic healing arts	Relationships
Awareness	Horses	Remorse
Bitterness	Humility	Resentment
Blockages	Illness	Scapegoats
Caves	Instinct	Self-mastery
Centaurs	Intellect	Self-sacrifice
Compassion	Integration	Service
Completion	Keys	Shamans
Consciousness	Mind/body connection	Spiritual growth
Contribution	Mavericks	Suffering
Cynicism	Medicine	Teachers
Depression	Mentors	Transformation
Disappointment	Mortality	Transcendence
Disillusionment	Originality	Turning point
Divine child	Passageways	Understanding
Empathy	Patience	Unity
Failings	Peace	Unresolved issues
Flaws	Perceptions	Wellness
Guilt	Personal growth	Will
Healers/healing/health	Quests	Wisdom
Higher consciousness	Reinvention	Wounding

Traveling Companions

Julia Child

From 1963 to 1973, Julia Child produced a weekly cooking show called *The French Chef*, which was broadcast on Public Television Station WGBH in Boston, Massachusetts. In this series, Julia offered her vast repertoire of experience and skills in French cooking to countless American cooks, by teaching them how to cook in the French way.

Diane

"She had such a love of life that she wasn't afraid of dying," said those of her friends who knew her best. Diane was diagnosed with fourth-stage breast cancer at age thirty-seven. Her twelve-year journey with the disease ended at the age of fifty. In attendance at her funeral were three hundred volunteer members of the Diane Z. Breast Cancer Support Group. Diane founded the organization while she was battling the disease, to provide support and education to women newly diagnosed with breast cancer. In the face of her own mortality, she offered her contribution to her community

and, with it, a legacy of love, mentorship, support, education, and compassion.

Mother Teresa

"…Mother Teresa too had 'many a sacrifice ready' for her in the decades to come. She was fifty years old and was about to begin a new phase in spreading her mission of love that would take her on numerous journeys around the world. … These trips would exact their price in time, fatigue and public speaking and serve as further proof of her love."

From *Mother Teresa: Come Be My Light: The Private Writings of the "Saint of Calcutta,"* edited and with commentary by Brian Kolodiejchuk, M.C.

Mary

"It began as my own personal journey. My mother and aunts all died of breast cancer, making me at high risk for the disease." With this awareness, Mary, a licensed acupuncturist, expanded her professional repertoire by training in the use of a leading edge breast cancer screening technology called digital infrared thermal imaging.

While using it in her private practice, a magazine article was written about her work with this new diagnostic tool, thus getting the word out to many more people than was possible solely through her professional practice. In the article, she was quoted as saying, "We have one more arrow in our quiver. The days of blind trust and blind faith in our orthodox medical system are over. We need to take responsibility for our own health."

KIM

"Lexus is my professional family and I care about everyone there like I do my personal family." As the oldest child of four, Kim was the family nurturer. She refused any attention for herself, and instead, selflessly cared for each member of her family, even into adulthood.

At the age of forty, Kim went to work for an automobile dealership, whose representation included Lexus cars. At the age of fifty, Kim was elected by her peers to represent the Central Division in the National Lexus Commitment to Perfection Program. In this position, Kim taught customer care and satisfaction skills to the national network of Lexus employees. Her work in this capacity touched 11,830 individuals across the United States. She became one of the most popular trainers with her repertoire of personal development skills, natural empathy, and selflessness.

AL

Al was working on a 200 million dollar proposal for one of his clients when the tingling sensation in his right arm began. After only two minutes into the stress test administered in the emergency room, the doctor immediately admitted him to the hospital. Forty-eight hours later, he underwent quintuple bypass heart surgery.

After the operation, a cardiologist prescribed a battery of medications that he would have to take for the rest of his life. Al fired the doctor. "As far as I was concerned, I had no choice but to change." That same sentiment was put to him very succinctly by a good friend who told him, "Do it or die." That night,

Al made a pact with himself to improve his diet, heal the broken relationships in his life, and eliminate work-induced stress, even if it meant changing his career.

He threw away the anti-depressants that had been prescribed for him and made a visit to a psychiatrist, who suggested he read a book by Tony Robbins, a pioneer in life coaching. Soon after that, Al began attending Robbins's seminars, where he was able to transform his anger and confusion. For the past eleven years, he has volunteered at Tony Robbins's seminars all over the United States, using his newfound heart-centered empowerment skills to facilitate personal transformation in program participants.

Alas for those that never sing, but die with all their music in them!

Oliver Wendell Holmes

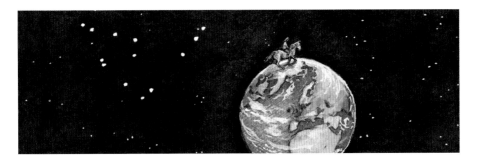

McKenzie's Journal

December 23, 2002 • I am tucked into seat 11C on a flight bound for Michigan. I look at my watch to see that it's almost noon. I'm about to turn fifty years old at 37,000 feet of altitude. I mentally review the phone call I received yesterday from my mother (actually, she's calling for my father who wants to avoid speaking to me, especially under the circumstances.) She usually calls me once a year to chat for a few minutes, which feels to me as if she does so out of either obligation or guilt. This time, she called to ask for money to save them from a self-inflicted financial crisis. Forget a relationship, just the money, please.

Because of my understanding of Chiron, I know that at this time of my Chiron Return I can fall back into a wounding situation with them. I need to step back, reflect, and review Melanie Reinhart's book, *Chiron and the Healing Journey*. It will help me to make wise choices based upon both the facts and feelings of my particular Chiron wound that for me, pertains to my parents. I am determined to do the right thing for them, even if it might not be the easy thing.

My father and I have been estranged for twenty-three years, but the rift widened in 1985; when I started to date Bill, my father turned on me with even more animosity. At the time, Bill held a challenging and fulfilling corporate position—something that my father had failed to realize in his own career when he was about fifty-one. My father's tyrannical disposition had spoiled his opportunity for advancement into a vice-presidency at the company he was then working for in Chicago. Bill, on the other hand, was likeable, with a flexible management style for which he was respected, appreciated, and even loved by his employees and co-workers.

From my knowledge of astrological cycles, I know that the timing of my mother's phone call is universal clock-perfect. I've done a lot of work in the past years to become conscious of my Chiron wound. Awareness of it eased the anxiety that I always felt around my father but could never put into words.

My father had used me as a model in his commercial illustration business in Chicago from the age of five until my last, and fateful, photo shoot (pun intended) at the age of nineteen. In my first job I posed as a ballerina (and a ballerina I was not) touching my toes next to an empty carton of Borden's Milk. Wearing that outfit was an unnatural—no, hellish experience—for the tough, little tomboy that I was then. Each subsequent shoot fortunately freed me from school, but unfortunately delivered me into the hands of hairdressers and perfume-laden Saks Fifth Avenue sales ladies. They gleefully conspired with my father to make me into Daddy's pretty little girl-model. I hated dresses. I hated hairdos even more. I much preferred wearing any sort of dirt and havocked hair. Nevertheless, Daddy dictated a clean, carefully composed female image for purchase by prominent corporations for those fourteen, formative years of my life. *Life Magazine*, the *Chicago Tribune*, Borden Milk, and others carried that image around in their pages and on the sides of their trucks throughout the city of Chicago. Daddy's moods soared when his creative acts reaped recognition; but his moods went straight to hell (taking everyone with him) when things weren't so well received.

According to Reinhart, the first Chiron event is typified as wounding at the hands of parents, teachers, or other authority figures. In my life map, Chiron, the wounded healer, is located in the area of one's career, parents, status, and visibility. With my astrological computer program, I determine that the exact window of time that this occurred was May 5, 1971 to November 7, 1972.

It was right on schedule, and I remember it well: in October 1972, my father called to tell me to get myself out of my Animal Science class at the University of Illinois and come to McCormick Place in Chicago. I was nineteen years old with a long history with Chiron and my father. This is how my wounding played out:

> Paper backdrop. Little girl. Five-year old innocent is picked up, placed just so. Told not to move. Instead, she doesn't breathe. Surrounded and stared down by hot lights baking her skin to china. As he barks, people scurry with cameras, props and costumes. They spin a media web of illusion around her—and into her consciousness. A woman steps behind her with scissors, cuts the outfit open up the back, and band-aids it back together with masking tape to produce artificial perfection for the camera. They will never know. An empty cardboard carton of Borden's milk at her feet—empty of the real thing. They will never know.
>
> The domineering art director shouts, "touch your toes and hold your breath on the count of three!"
>
> He is her father. He is both threatening and threatened because today, his image rides on her performance. She is his circus horse. She tightens with anxiety in a pose of painful perfection while trying to appear carefree and vital because she drinks Borden's milk. In truth, she is frightened for her life. But they will never know.
>
> Cameras click wildly to replace reality with fantasy. "Yes! " He exclaims. It goes well for him. His fame is her famine. She is money in the bank, not the daughter in his heart.
>
> Now she is nineteen. Long, blonde, model hair. Yearning for what is real. Girl-woman wounded countless times by the art director's artillery. Girl-woman dying for illusion's sake— for his sake. He calls

to take her out of university classes. "Be at McCormick Place this afternoon. You'll be modeling basketball uniforms for Wilson Sporting Goods." She does not yet know, but her soul does, that this will be the last time for fakery. Her human imperfections, suffocating in the dark, beg for the light of day to breathe.

On the way, she stops at an anonymous salon. Scissors declare the long, blonde, model hair, commandeered by him, free—for her sake.

Then, and only then, does she face the retail representatives, set designers, photographers, lighting crew—and him—waiting for her long, blonde, model hair. She was late because she had to stop and find herself on the way.

The long, blonde, model hair is gone, dashing his camera's fantasy. All hell breaks loose. His fury sends torrents of muddy water over her, polluting her fertile feelings with the scum of Irish tyranny. He spews shame on her, here, on the stage of illusion, set by the players of retail sales. Her father fires her, but only after she must pose in the pain of public humiliation one last time. In the face of the fear of rejection, she had unconsciously found a way to fling her flaws at him so that he would never want to point his camera at her again. And her soul? It sang all the way back to the university farm.

Years and healing later, she is a woman who is kissed by sun and earth and water and horses and dogs. Her clothes aren't faked with masking tape. She gets out of bed each morning with havocked blonde hair and unconditional love for herself—and for him.

I have spent the years since this first Chiron wounding experience "healing into awareness" before I even knew that an archetypal Chiron existed in me. Since then, through my training in transpersonal psychology, astrology, mythology, and mind/body medicine, Chiron has become an important part of my personal life and professional counseling practice.

What about my second major Chiron event? Reinhart says that it typically offers the first suggestion about the meaning of one's life, as well as presents an opportunity to bring both sides of one's nature (intellect and instinct) together in a balanced way.

So, keep on keeping on living the life which your inner voice directs, kindly, lovingly: giving help wherever you can, giving love and sustenance to this great work of illuminating all life. Your life is like a pebble dropped into a pool of water, creating ripples endlessly. You do not know the end of a word, a thought, an action.

White Eagle

I calculate the "window" in which it occurred: July 31, 1989 to May 22, 1990. Oh, yes. At that time, I was thirty-six and thirty-seven years old, living in Japan, and discovering Eastern religious traditions and metaphysics. I was also exploring higher consciousness in the experience of the Higher Self, and using the work to, among many other things, seek a balance between my mind and body. This was absolutely the first suggestion about the meaning of my life, and even though I didn't realize it then, it coincided with my Second Call.

According to Reinhart again, the third major Chiron event can potentially be a very creative time. It can give one a sense of one's place in life. My third Chiron event happened between December 7, 1995 and August 27, 1996. I was living both in Santa Fe and at the cabin, facilitating individuals from diverse ethnic, cultural, social, economic, and educational backgrounds in making a conscious connection to the Higher Self—to find within themselves the high road upon which they could live their lives in awareness of who they were and why they were here.

At that time, I traveled to Bali with some classmates from Nine Gates Mystery School. With David Patten as our teacher and guide, we explored Balinese culture, arts, religious traditions, and our dreams.

As part of the program, we visited an esteemed Balinese woodcarver, Ida Bagus Astina. Under his instruction, we carved our own pieces in his outdoor studio. Later that day, as we were leaving, I noticed a particular carving on the back wall of the studio along with some others. Ida told me that they had been hanging there for almost a year. No doubt. They were covered with several layers of dust.

The piece that had caught my eye was a long vertical carving, in hibiscus wood, of a woman being seized by the crown of her head by an eagle. This was the very same image and experience that I had in a Higher Self session in 1992, when I was thirty-nine years old. Ida, who was a Hindu, had come up with the exact same image for this carving in 1994!

It was a compelling confirmation that all people—no matter how seemingly separated by time, distance, culture, walk of life, or religious tradition—can access the same archetypal images from the "universal well," using these images for healing, awareness, and creativity.

Healing, awareness, and creativity are Chiron themes. In this, my third Chiron event, life was giving me a direct experience of "right here, in this experience, is who you are." At this key juncture, the universal clock was awakening me to the meaning of my life, just as it does, has done, and will always do for everyone.

Most importantly, I had traveled halfway around the world for this experience. Now, my memorable childhood dream at age eleven takes on even more meaning; in that dream, the colorful globe of the world that stood in the corner of my school classroom was suspended in the middle of a star-filled universe. In it, I was riding my horse, Button Up, (the horse a symbol for the Centaur Chiron) over the top of the globe, from country to country. The dream at that young age was life's first hint to me of my life-to-be. There, in the wood carver's studio in Bali, the dream was made manifest.

Needless to say, I had to have this woodcarving as a symbol of whom I was becoming—a teacher and facilitator of holistic (Chiron) healing modalities.

Ida agreed to sell me his carving, which I carried back home, halfway around the world.

Now, I am fifty years old and Chiron has returned in its orbit to the exact location in the sky where it was on the day of my birth. The Chiron Return is that point in life (based upon the consciousness that one has acquired thus far) that will be problematic or bring a positive direction to one's life—or a bit of both. Back to my parents….

December 24, 2002 • I research my horoscope to obtain more detail about the meaning, pitfalls, and potentials of my Chiron theme. On the day of my birth, December 23, 1952, Chiron was located at eleven degrees in the sign of Capricorn, which, in my case, was the Tenth House. The Tenth House is the domain of career, public visibility, status, and parents. This means that, for me, both my wounding and the eventual contribution that I will offer, will occur in the domain of career, public visibility, status, and/ or parents.

Depending on the unique configuration of a person's life map, or horoscope, Chiron will be found in a specific area of each life in the same way. Most of the time, but not always, Chiron will have one or more additional aspects, or characteristics. These characteristics add more details to one's Chiron "story."

I refer to Melanie Reinhart's book, *Chiron and the Healing Journey*, and paraphrase from it:

My Chiron pitfalls:

- Living the unfulfilled ambitions of my father. (too many times and in all the wrong places)
- Difficulty in setting and achieving goals and finding my professional place in society. (oooh, that word g-o-a-l)
- Having many false starts in my search for my vocation. (about a million false starts, it seemed)

- Experiencing feelings of failure, no matter how successful I appeared, because of setting impossible standards for myself. (recognize this much?)

- Struggling under the burden of parental expectations that can never be fulfilled, trying to succeed where they failed, or reach goals they did not realize. (understatement of the year)

- Clinging to role playing and external facades in order to conceal my vulnerability and feelings of being out of place. (an energy drain to the max)

- Assuming responsibility for things over which I have no control. (ooops.)

- Needing to abandon my futile dealings with the difficulties of others that have nothing to do with me. ("it's none of my business" is my new mantra, especially with regard to my parents right now)

- Carrying others' burdens, hoping for reward or recognition in return. (I did this to a ridiculous extent in the past, but since healed it with the realization that I am not a beast of burden and besides, the price for being one exceeds any reward.)

- Misjudging my own capacities, taking on too much, failing, and then feeling guilty for not living up to sky-high standards. (those hurt!)

- Feeling conspicuous in a position of authority and sabotaging myself on the threshold of success. (how many times?)

- Wounding relationship with my father and the father archetype in general. (my task was to engage my own kind and wise authority)

- Authoritarian or negative father speaks loudly within my own psyche and threatens the positive outcome of conscious goals I may be striving for. I need to have the courage to face my own wounds first. (whatever requires courage, go there immediately)

- Having jobs or circumstances with a great deal of responsibility, but not being able to take in nourishment from life. (breast cancer taught me how to nourish myself)

My Chiron potentials:

- Finding joy in climbing the mountain of my own aspirations.

- Nurturing the qualities of dignity, presence, and self-containment.

- Eventually realizing success from a healthy sense of self-respect and self-worth, rather than success as a compensation for a lack of it.

- Having a natural sense of authority and dignity that invites respect from others.

- Healing the wounding effects of an early relationship with my mother to become a good mother to myself.

- The ability to foster the growth of others by re-parenting them, showing love and giving the guidance that may have not have been given them otherwise.

- Can take seriously my responsibilities toward myself, and be unafraid to struggle with difficulties in my life that others might avoid in theirs.

My additional Chiron characteristics:

- Experiencing rude awakenings to my mortal limits, but having an ability to bounce back from illnesses, personal tragedies, and crises of faith. (broken pelvis from riding my cousin's bike into the truck, broken collarbone from Button Up falling on me after I fell off her over a jump, shoulder surgery from way too much racquetball, Bill's suicide, Diane's death, the loss of Ciao, and breast cancer to name just a few)

- Relationships become a means of connection to realms of higher consciousness or an experience of social or cultural expansion. (the many countries that Bill and I traveled to, as well as Santa Fe)

- Possessing a capacity to teach and inspire others and to assist them in finding meaning in their own lives. (yes, and grateful for this)

- Having a gift for articulating an overview of situations, being able to bring out the best in people, as well as to help them articulate their highest aspirations. (double yes, double gratitude)

- A positive outlook on life and trust in its bounty inspires others. (triple yes, triple gratitude)

- My sense of hope, optimism, and confidence in life's possibilities may have been crushed as a child. (Fortunately, I had a well of optimism within myself that was deeper than the wound)

- Carrying the accumulated, unconscious, and repressed religious aspirations of my ancestors, I journey through extremes to find my True Self. (the potato fields of Ireland...

and it's nice to have a sweet, Italian mother to counterbalance the Irish father)

- Repeated disillusionments yield the rediscovering of my own inner spiritual authority. (I make a toast to whatever it took to get there)

- Possessing a strong intuition with intimations of the future, but challenged in bringing lofty ideas into form. (would rather talk than bring things into form)

- A combination of mountain heights and psychological depths. (this shoe fits this Capricorn)

- Being compelled to find a philosophy of personal meaning that befits my own life experience. (ongoing)

- The comfort of belonging to a collectively accepted religion may be denied me, and this is both my wound and my challenge to access a deep, inner source of wisdom and guidance for myself. (oh, the thrill of the chase)

- Finding the inner Teacher. (Norbu Sherpa)

- Being a seeker after truth. (nothing wrong with this up to a point in the journey where you realize that you no longer have to seek after what you already know—you just have to know where to find it)

- Being dedicated to global causes. (what would this world be like if every single person on earth lived their higher life purpose? How to contribute toward that end?)

- Committing to the path of integration and wholeness. (the long and winding road)

- Going on quests, journeys, and pilgrimages that are productive for healing and inner growth. (The dream, as an eleven year old, of riding my horse all over the world: the interpretation of which I now understand as healing myself and facilitating healing and awareness in others through an elevated worldview that is obtained by both outer world travel and "inner world" travels with the Higher Self.)

- Willing to reflect deeply on my experiences, to balance expansion with enough introspection and stillness so that integration can be reached. (sitting still has never been easy for me, but the insights gained are worth it!)

The pitfalls and potentials of a Chiron characteristic that I share collectively with everyone born between February 2, 1952 and November 14, 1989:

- Exploring the bridge between the personal and higher mind, but must not allow preoccupation with the large picture to distract me from the elements of my personal life.

- Coming to terms with powerful collective issues by elevating my consciousness.

- Moderating the desire for freedom from constraints by discovering that I am already free.

- Being apt to make sudden changes.

- Being thrown into unexpected and unwelcome events.

- Embracing new ideas and new ways of living.

- Being an original thinker.

- Being able to perceive situations with penetrating insight.

- Knowing that my insights may make others feel uncomfortable as I regard life from a position of nonattachment.

- Discovering that the wound may be a lack of connection with my personal feelings as well as the disillusionment felt when life fails to live up to my ideal plan.

- Thriving on change and experience, whether or not I consciously seek it.

- Going out on a limb to courageously try new things, even in the face of ridicule and lack of support from others.

- Being vigilant that I do not become too brittle or inflexible, unable to change course, or flow with the tides of necessity.

- Allowing my true creative capacities to take form once I have found and accepted my own inner discipline and boundaries.

- Being unable to accept a higher authority other than my own personal voice, thereby adding new sufferings, for part of the journey, to those I already have, until I am able to hear that higher Voice.

- Learning that freedom is found within.

- Stepping beyond the cultural, and sometimes wounding, mental conditioning to birth my own original ideas, which demands great discipline.

- Being an agent of change.

- Seeing and understanding the map of my life and its perfect symmetry. These visions stay with me throughout the rest of my life, encouraging me to obey and follow what I have seen.

- Giving birth to the new without indiscriminately rejecting the old, a powerful intuitive sense, with a capacity for compassionate nonattachment from emotionally laden ideas and situations, and a deep understanding of the process of creative thinking.

- Strongly activating the process of individuation, which in turn catalyzes major changes in lifestyle.

- Seeking help in a significant teacher or teaching.

- Renewing my sense of personal meaning and/or realization of vocation to find connection with a sense of purpose.

- Having various kinds of inner experiences that lead me to an appreciation of the underlying unity of all life beyond the dualism that I normally call reality. This kind of experience promotes healing, and understanding that the denial of it may behind the symptoms of any illness.

- Confronting my mortality and finding that an acceptance of death transforms my attitude toward life.

I am grateful for Melanie Reinhart's work; it has helped me to discover my Chiron contribution from the outside in. And, I am in awe of the childhood dream that offered me the first symbolic hint of my life-to-be, the symbolism of which has been revealed as I have lived my purpose. It is no wonder then, why this dream, of all the dreams I have ever had, has stayed with me so tenaciously throughout my life; it is steadfast because life is steadfast in support of purpose.

True power is wisdom found in remembering your total journey. Wisdom comes from remembering the pathway that you have walked in another person's moccasins. Compassion, caring, teaching, loving and sharing your gifts, talents and abilities are the gateway to power.

From "The Horse," Chapter 35 in "Medicine Cards," by Jamie Sams

I am also grateful to the first Chiron wounding in my first "career" as my father's photographic model; it set me on my path toward wholeness. And last, my heart is heavy as I realize that the most painful experience of Chiron was not my own—it was Bill's death as a result of his Chiron wound.

It's up to me to determine my contribution at this time of my Chiron Return. And there's a wonderful way for me to find it—find Norbu.

Birdsong brings relief to my longing.
I am just as ecstatic as they are,
But with nothing to say!
Please, universal soul,
Practice some song or something through me!

Jalaluddin Rumi

Sherpa Norbu's Parable

"I know it's here somewhere," Norbu murmurs to himself as he peers inside dusty boxes and tattered envelopes. Finally, he remembers where to look for it. He feels around the back of one of the wooden wall sections for a certain peg. Unhooking an object from it, he holds it up to a shaft of light coming in through the roof vent. Rubbing away a thick layer of dust from its surface, he inspects it carefully; suspended from a loop of seven strands of hair from a centaur's mane, hangs a key as ancient as the heavens. Norbu gently cups both hands around it and holds it to his heart.

• • •

Here at the summit, Shaypa requests permission to enter my yurt. As she pulls back the flap, a female bluebird bursts from my hands, darting past Shaypa through the doorway.

At first she is startled, but Shaypa's curiosity quickly leads her back outside to follow it. The little bird has settled on the top of a post anchored in the snow. Strung along the post are faded, threadbare flags of blue, green, white, yellow, and red. Shaypa, with her love of horses, loves that these prayer flags are called lungta—windhorses—named for the images of horses placed in the center of each. As the wind blows through the flags, the horses carry out to the world prayers of blessing and compassion.

Shaypa watches and listens intently as the bird, perched lightly on the post, begins to sing. She notices how natural it is for her to sing. She doesn't sing because it's a job. She sings because the song is coming from her Being.

There is no shelter here; this tiny bird is exposed and vulnerable to the wind, snow, rain, lightning, and thunder. The elements are not always kind to her, but she keeps singing, no matter what the conditions.

She sings as it begins to snow. She responds to the snow with the song, just as she would respond to the rain or thunder or lightning. She sings to calm or chaos, too. She offers the song to it all.

She never changes when the song changes—she's stays pretty much the same. She may cock her head when a different quality of sound comes through, or she may change her stance to accommodate different notes, but she remains as the bird that she very much is.

She sings the song by allowing it to simply come through her. Even though there's not much to her fluffy body, it's amazing what comes through her. The beauty and largesse of the song and its effects do not match her tiny body. It is a mystery how something so large can come so perfectly through something so small. All she does is open her body and it comes through.

The song meets the thunder, giving it magnitudes more beauty, until the thunder itself becomes a song. And as she sings into wind, it too becomes a song. The rain becomes the song as well, and as it waters the earth, the earth becomes the song. This little bird changes the world with the song.

The post is very solid, almost tree-like. Its edges have been softened by the elements; its grayed fibers are old and separating. But this post gives no hint of collapse. It is steadfast and reliable, no matter the conditions. Its support is eternal.

This post has seen a lot of birds like this little bird in its time. Not only does it support her, but its own life is supported and sustained by the bird. The post and this little bird are engaged in an important relationship; she has a place to sing from and the post gains life from the song.

The song sends a vibration to the base of the post, drawing countless beings to it. These beings are not residents, but pilgrims. They, and others coming before and after them, are timeless travelers. A kind of cross-fertilization takes place as they meet each other, and this creates great vitality in them.

The song is a calling, but not a calling out. She doesn't sing to bring the beings to her; the beings come to the song she sings. And all of this happens by virtue of the song coming through a tiny bluebird perched atop a post!

Well, that was her day life, but now it's night. It becomes very quiet. The moon hangs in the sky among the stars, casting a soft glow over her. She does two things: she waits and she rests. She waits for the return of daylight as her cue to sing—by resting!

She sleeps with her head down, feathers tucked in, eyes closed, breathing deeply. She surrenders to sleep. She sleeps perfectly because she knows why she must sleep. She sleeps in order to be able to sing. It's essential that she sleep, essential that she become a bird again, in concert with her life as an instrument for the song. This is a very purposeful rest. Look how she safeguards it. She rests as well as she sings. Her rest makes perfect the song.

She does not know what song will come through when the dawn comes. She is never invested in what comes through her. She may be amazed at what songs come, but she is never attached to them. Non-attachment is essential; the moment she gets attached to the song everything stops. If she starts thinking or worrying about the song, she will obstruct the birth of the song. She will prevent the world from becoming the song. Simply put, she has to let go of every song, and never wish for it again. She must return to utter openness and await the next song.

So, being a smart bird, she simply keeps her body open to whatever song comes, being amazed and delighted with each, but never preferring any song over another. She knows that each song gives to the world whatever the world needs.

There is a tiny little heart that beats inside of her. The flow of the song is what keeps her heart beating. That's how she lives.

Oh, but, there is a wound in her heart! This wound resides not only in her heart, but also in the hearts of all birds. The wound bleeds into the song. It seems so sad to hear her wound as she sings into the world. But then, if you listen carefully, you hear devotion. Her wound brings devotion to the song! And because this is so, she doesn't try to hold back her wound from bleeding into the song.

The song and the wound are so unified that you cannot tell them apart. Together, they change the wind. And the wind becomes a song that brings the clouds. Together they change the rain. And the rain becomes a song that offers its gift to dry earth. Together they change the thunder. And the thunder becomes a song that drums a new heartbeat for the world. Together, the song and the wound change the snow at the summit. And the snow melts and flows from its Source, bringing life. And all of this by virtue of a tiny wounded bluebird and a song.

Shaypa blinks and rubs her eyes. Then, she remembers that she has left me in the yurt! But, the moment she turns back to me, I appear—it is she and I, together under the brilliant, blue sky.

"It's in the yurt," I tell her, without needing to hear her question.

Shaypa's eyes widen in awe, but not surprise. I have always known her thoughts.

She excuses herself and slips quietly into the yurt. It takes a moment for her eyes to adjust. Shafts of light stream down from the roof vent, creating an intricate interplay of light and shadow on the floor and walls.

On my altar are sacred objects carefully laid out on a woven cloth. She kneels down to inspect them as thin trails of burning incense curl up through the roof opening.

At the far end of my altar lies a book and, for a moment, she stares at it wondering what it is. Scriptures? My diary? Hmmmnn. Shaypa hesitates, and then carefully picks it up. She ducks back outside, eager to tell me that she has found what I assured her was there. She returns just in time to see me step off the summit. I do not look back.

A shadow races across the snow. Shaypa looks up to see the eagle diving straight for me, its talons in full extension. It seizes me by the crown of my head, pulling me up into the empty space under its wings.

The pages of the book that Shaypa is holding whip wildly in the gusting winds and she holds them to protect them from being torn away. As she does so, she notices the words on one page:

"The eagle seizes Shaypa by the crown of her head, pulling her skyward. She suddenly sees the world she once knew transformed into another. Once it is certain that her vision is as clear as its own, the eagle releases her, inviting her to fly with it."

The eagle makes a last pass over the summit. As it spirals upward, the air under its wings becomes a song. A resonant voice, neither male nor female but a perfect unity of both, tells Shaypa, "This is the song of Love. What I am is what you are, and have always been, since the beginning of the Beginning."

In Dream

Dear love,
What other days
unstructured in our present,
beckon beyond the borders of our sight?

On the surface of our moments
do we live,
our eyes upon the road of time.
So firm the focus that directs our minds,
We do not glance aside
to catch the whispered promise
of our dreams.
To such strange land
our prejudiced perception
holds no passport.

And yet in gossamer thickets do we wander,
and dip our consciousness
inside pools of experience,
unknowing that we move
through dimensions strange to
our waking selves.

What vapour chair supports our dreaming form,
that eyes do not perceive in morning's light?
Our bodies lie supine upon the bed,
and yet we move through midnight mansions
careless of closed doors,
at once an adult and a child.

In dream
we crack the canopy of Time,
and fling aside the focus
of our waking thought.

Winging outward into far tomorrows
and distant yesterdays
our moments go,
as dawn flies before the sun,
The self we know
a changeling.

Dear love,
what ghostly counterpart,
rejected on our waking,
seeks to tell us
of alternate ways, unstructured days,
no longer captured in a cage
of Time?

CHERRY EARLE, NEW ZEALAND

EPILOGUE

I, Shaypa, stand on the summit watching the eagle circle overhead with the spirit of Norbu Sherpa in the empty space under its wings. This book lies in my open hands. The wind suddenly picks up the pages, flapping them in every direction, like prayer flags sending compassion to every corner of the world.

Norbu once told me that some climbers stay at the summit too long. He said that new life is gained by letting go of the old. My new life is not found here at the summit. It is found in letting go of the summit. So I remain for only a few moments to gaze at a vista that extends farther than I can humanly see.

Norbu's yak-skin boots lie nearby in the snow. The felt uppers, on which crescent moons are embroidered all the way around, are well worn but not, by any means, worn out. What a beautiful metaphor they are for a life fulfilled by purpose.

When I pull them on, I find that even though they are still too big for my feet, I can walk in them well enough. It just means that even though I've reached this summit, my journey is not over. If I take to heart the lessons I have learned from my ascent—to remain awake, aware, and willing—my feet will eventually grow to fill them.

I ask Norbu's boots for direction as I take my first step off the summit. The boots will know the terrain when I don't. I can really trust these boots. These boots are all I need to take me to my Third Call and beyond.

I step off the summit and discover that all of the experiences I have had on this journey converge into one light that shines outward from my heart into the world. It is a brilliant light that illuminates the way forward. I can never be lost now.

Walking toward base camp, I notice luminous diamonds scattered over the mountainside. Some lay partially buried in the snow, still undiscovered. Others have been abandoned. Still others mark the graves of fallen climbers whose summits have been attained where they lay. Where did all these diamonds come from?

I have walked that long road to freedom. I have tried not to falter. I have made missteps along the way. But I have discovered the secret that after climbing a great hill, one only finds that there are many more hills to climb. I have taken a moment here to rest, to steal a view of a glorious vista that surrounds me, to look back on the distance I have come. But I can rest only for a moment, for with freedom comes responsibilities, and I dare not linger, for my long walk is not yet ended.

— Nelson Mandela

Suddenly, I remember the six-pointed star Norbu had given to me at my Second Call. When I reach into my left shirt pocket to retrieve it, I find a diamond instead. Its six facets reflect Courage, Determination, Devotion, Strength, Enthusiasm, and Focus— the attributes of my True Being that came forth as I accepted my authenticity, power, clarity, stature, balance and beliefs, and contribution. I now see midlife for what it really is—an opportunity to thrive for the rest of my life.

Traveler's FAQ's

How can I obtain a hard copy of my personal life map?

Any qualified astrologer can draw one up for you. They will need the exact date, location, and time of your birth. You can also obtain one from me, through my website at www.guideformidlife.com.

If I already have a hard copy of my life map or can supply the exact date, location, and time of my birth, what additional information is available to me about my specific midlife crises?

You can access:

- The beginning and ending dates for each crisis
- The specific areas of your life in which each crisis occurs
- The general types of experiences that tend to occur in each area
- Guidance on how to navigate each crisis, based upon the specifics of your life map

How can I obtain the exact time of my birth if it's not on my birth certificate?

Write to the hospital at which you were born. They often require a nominal fee for records research and postage.

If I cannot obtain my exact time of birth, what then?

The Travel Itinerary and Sights and Sounds sections of this book will still give you great information and guidance based solely upon the year of your birth.

I don't want to, or can't obtain a hard copy of my life map, but I do want guidance for my midlife or other personal challenges. Can you provide that?

Absolutely. My higher life purpose is to counsel, guide, and teach. Just contact me through the website to set up an appointment.

I want to make the connection with my Higher Self! How can I arrange for this work?

The Deva Foundation, Santa Fe, New Mexico, is the Foundation at which I trained.

They provide facilitation, as well as conduct workshops devoted to personal and spiritual growth. They can also put you in touch with a Deva facilitator in or near your area.

The Deva Foundation can be contacted at www.deva.org.

Are you available for lectures, study groups, seminars, motivational speaking, and conferences?

Yes to all. Just go to the website www.guideformidlife.com for more information.

I love the illustrations in your book! Are they for sale as reproductions?

Yes. Glenn's work may be purchased on the website.

Where can I find more information?

www.guideformidlife.com

About the Author

McKenzie Magee is an international facilitator of psycho-spiritual integration, a method that accesses the Higher Self. As a teacher and counselor, she has sixteen years experience in guiding individuals committed to their personal growth and life purpose.

McKenzie was educated in science, psychology, and world spiritual traditions under the guidance of esteemed academic and spiritual teachers. She has lived abroad and has traveled internationally as a motivational speaker, workshop leader, and lecturer.

She includes Eastern and Western wisdom traditions, transpersonal psychology, a wide range of holistic healing modalities, and astrology in her professional counseling practice, Higher Ground, Inc.

McKenzie is a professional member of the Association of Transpersonal Psychology, the Institute of Noetic Sciences, and is an alumnus of Nine Gates Mystery School and the Deva Foundation.

McKenzie is available for lectures, motivational speaking engagements, workshops, study groups, and personal consultations.

You can contact her through her website at www.guideformidlife.com

BIBLIOGRAPHY

Melanie Reinhart, *Chiron and the Healing Journey:*
An Astrological and Psychological Perspective, 1989
The Penguin Group, Penguin Books Ltd., England

Rex E. Bills, *The Rulership Book*, 1971
American Federation of Astrologers, Inc., Tempe, Arizona